# PEPPERCORN'S
# PACIFICS

PETER TUFFREY

GREAT NORTHERN

## ACKNOWLEDGEMENTS

In compiling this book I am grateful for the assistance received from the following people: Ben Brooksbank, Doug Brown, David Burrill, David Clay, Peter Crangle, David Dippie, David Dunn, Peter Jary, David Joy, John Law, Paul License, Hugh Parkin, Derek Porter, Richard Postill, Bill Reed, P.N. Townend, Andrew Warnes, Sue Warnes, Tony Watson.

Gratitude should also be expressed to my son Tristram for his general help and encouragement throughout the course of the project.

## PHOTOGRAPHS

Unless otherwise stated all photographs are from the collections of Ben Burrell or Malcolm Crawley. Every effort has been made to gain permission to use the images. If you feel you have not been contacted please let me know: petertuffrey@rocketmail.com.

## INFORMATION

I have taken reasonable steps to verify the accuracy of the information in this book but it may contain errors or omissions. Any information that may be of assistance to rectify any problems will be gratefully received. Please contact me by email petertuffrey@rocketmail.com or in writing: Peter Tuffrey, 8 Wrightson Avenue, Warmsworth, Doncaster, South Yorkshire, DN4 9QL.

---

Great Northern Books Limited
PO Box 1380, Bradford, BD5 5FB
www.greatnorthernbooks.co.uk



ISBN: 978-1-912101-70-2

Design and layout: David Burrill

CIP Data
A catalogue for this book is available from the British Library

# FOREWORD

## BY MARK ALLATT

### THE A1 STEAM LOCOMOTIVE TRUST

Unlike most people writing forewords for such learned texts, I'm not of an age to have experienced LNER steam in anything but the preservation era. I'm not sure when I first became obsessed with the LNER and its fine locomotives but I'm sure that it was not helped by the receipt of a Triang-Hornby 'Flying Scotsman' Train Set at Christmas 1970 aged five. It probably didn't help being taken to see no. 532 *Blue Peter* at Barrow Hill Roundhouse, not far from where I was brought up in Dronfield, North Derbyshire, in 1971, following her renaming on the BBC Blue Peter TV programme at Doncaster Works. What I didn't realise until more recently was that this connection goes back even further to a visit by no. 4472 *Flying Scotsman* to Sheffield in 1967 when I was around 18 months old. Family cine-camera footage clearly shows me as a babe in arms and the very distinctive image of fireman Dave Court with his mane of blonde hair on the footplate who I was to get to know well some 40 years later.

**Mark Allatt with no. 60163 *Tornado* at Darlington on the 'First Moves' weekend, August 2008.** Picture by Peter Neesam courtesy The A1 Steam Locomotive Trust.

Not being from a railway-interested family – my maternal grandfather worked on both the LMS and the LNER but died a few days before I was born – I didn't have any connections with the various LNER locomotive preservation societies and so I had to wait until my early 20s before joining The Gresley Society and The A4 Locomotive Society and attempting to get involved. In the meantime, I read voraciously everything I could find out about the locomotives of Gresley, Thompson and Peppercorn and started a collection of 'OO' gauge LNER models that continues to grow to this day.

Having finished university and with a bit more money in my pocket I was able to experience some of these magnificent locomotives first-hand, travelling over the Settle & Carlisle Railway behind no. 4472 *Flying Scotsman*, no. 4498 *Sir Nigel Gresley*, no. 4771 *Green Arrow* and of course no. 60532 *Blue Peter*. Latterly I was privileged to be on 'The Elizabethan' from London King's Cross to Peterborough on 24th October 1994 behind no. 60009 *Union of South Africa* and no. 4464 *Bittern's* 90mph runs on the East Coast Main Line in 2013. But I digress.

Although the LNER was a preservation pioneer, establishing its company museum in York following the Stockton & Darlington Railway centenary celebrations in 1925, the LNER fared badly in the preservation stakes following the rapid rundown of steam in the 1950s and 1960s. With both no. 4468 *Mallard* and no. 4771 *Green Arrow* on the list of locomotives to be preserved, even the world-famous *Flying Scotsman* would have headed for the scrapheap if Alan Pegler hadn't stepped in – so what hope was there for the less high profile Peppercorn Class A1s and A2s?

The Peppercorn Class A1s and A2s were designed by Arthur H. Peppercorn, the last Chief Mechanical Engineer of the LNER, with the first few built in the dying days of the LNER and the remainder by the newly nationalised British Railways. Thankfully Geoff Drury stepped in to rescue no. 60532 *Blue Peter* which had been withdrawn from service on the 31st December 1966 and put into store. *Blue Peter* was purchased for preservation in 1968 and with the involvement of the children's BBC TV programme of the same name, was restored to working condition once more. Restoration was undertaken at York, Leeds and Doncaster Works where it was repainted in LNER apple green livery as no. 532. 60,000 people witnessed its renaming by the BBC *Blue Peter* programme presenters at a Doncaster Works Open Day in 1971.

Sadly, there was no such happy ending for the Peppercorn Class A1s. Of the Peppercorn Class A1s, no. 60123 *H.A. Ivatt* was the first to go after it was involved in an accident near Offord in September 1962. Its classmates all followed between 1964 and 1966; the last to be withdrawn was no. 60145 *Saint Mungo*, from York in June 1966. It was sold to Draper's of Hull in August for breaking up – something that tragically took place after the failure of a bid by Geoff Drury to preserve the locomotive. And sadly, Albert Draper & Son Ltd was no Woodham Brothers Ltd of Barry Island. Its locomotives didn't linger long enough for preservationists to raise the funds to purchase and restore them as has happened to 213 locomotives from Woodham Bros and only one, Thompson class B1 no. 1264, was of LNER design. 29 Pacifics survived Barry, but due to its distance from the old LNER road, not a single Peppercorn Pacific was amongst them.

The fact that no Peppercorn Class A1s survived was enough of a clarion call to those who believed that a new one should be built, but in addition, a line of preserved East Coast Main Line express passenger locomotives from the 1890s until the end of steam, was broken by the absence of a Peppercorn Class A1 from 1966… until 2008.

*Blue Peter* did little work following the renaming until, in the late 1980s, Geoff Drury and NELPG reached an agreement for the group to restore the locomotive to main line condition. Restoration to BR Brunswick green livery as no. 60532 was carried out with assistance from ICI Wilton and the A2 was renamed by the BBC *Blue Peter* programme for a second time in December 1991. In early 1992 the locomotive obtained its main line certificate and then worked several railtours over routes such as the Settle & Carlisle Railway, and as far north as its old stomping ground of Aberdeen.

During this time, the locomotive worked very well and soon earned a reputation as a strong and reliable performer. However, on the 1st October 1994, whilst working a tour from Edinburgh to York the locomotive

**Dorothy Mather begins the construction of *Tornado* on 22nd April 1994 at BSD, Leeds.** Photograph by Ted Parker courtesy The A1 Steam Locomotive Trust.

suffered a major mechanical failure, caused by a prolonged uncontrolled wheel slip on departure from Durham station. During the slip both outside sets of valve gear were destroyed, the leading coupling rods were bent, all coupled wheel axle boxes were damaged and the left leading driving wheel moved on its axle. The repair work took 18 months to complete and the locomotive didn't resume its main line career until November 1996.

*Blue Peter's* main line certificate expired in September 2001 and with the locomotive based on the NYMR at the time, it remained in service there until the end of the 2002 season. no. 60532 was subsequently moved to Barrow Hill Roundhouse where it was repainted into the same apple green livery with 'British Railways' on the tender carried by no. 60163 *Tornado* and the two locomotives appeared together at several events, albeit with no. 60532 not in steam. The Drury family – Geoff Drury had passed away several years earlier - investigated various options to return *Blue Peter* to steam and in October 2014 the locomotive was sold to Jeremy Hosking's Royal Scot Locomotive & General Trust and is currently under overhaul to main line standards at LNWR Heritage in Crewe.

It has been said that the A1s were the finest express passenger locomotives ever built in Britain and 49 were built at Doncaster and Darlington in 1948/9 by British Railways. They worked over the whole of the East Coast Main Line, hauling up to 600 ton trains on schedules of a mile a minute. They were handsome and looked particularly elegant at the head of the Pullman expresses of the 1950s. However, the class was destined to have a very short life owing to rapid dieselisation with the first example withdrawn in 1962 and between then and 1966 the remainder followed.

And so, we fast forward to the late 1980s. The railway heritage movement had made great strides during the preceding 25 years. The ex-Barry restorations had grown more complex and ever more expensive. What not many years previously would have been considered as impossible projects were returning to steam - new driving wheels had been cast for King Class no. 6023 *King Edward II*, new cylinders for no. 71000 *Duke of Gloucester* and even entirely new steam locomotives built such as the replica *Locomotion No. 1* for the Stockton & Darlington Railway 150th Anniversary in 1975 and narrow gauge Ffestiniog Railway Double Fairlie *David Lloyd George*.

And so was born The A1 Steam Locomotive Trust with an ambitious mission to build a Peppercorn Class A1 Pacific for main line and preserved railway use. The Trust was launched at the Railway Institute in York in November 1990 with subsequent public meetings at King's Cross in March 1991 and Edinburgh later in the year. Unable to attend the York meeting, this precocious 25-year-old went along to the one at The Great Northern Hotel at King's Cross station. There I met the driving force behind the project, David Champion, who was to be its Chairman for the next ten years, and David Elliott and the late Barry Wilson who were to become the Director of Engineering and Finance Director respectively. And when the call went out for volunteers to help with marketing, PR and fundraising – and I worked in PR at the time – I put my hand up… and to this day I still lead these activities for the Trust.

The A1 Steam Locomotive Trust was established around four principles:

- *By using the best business practice by people experienced in the appropriate areas*
- *The application of simple funding methods capable of being understood and afforded by virtually anyone*
- *The enormity of the task demanded a mission statement: "The building and operation of an A1".*
- *The rules of the organisation to prohibit cliques and any forms of elitism.*

**No. 60163 takes shape in Darlington Locomotive Works in early 2000, with Bill Brown at the smokebox. The boiler would not arrive for several more years.** Picture by Phil Champion courtesy The A1 Steam Locomotive Trust.

Building *Tornado* was done from the original drawings but these were sometimes found to be incorrect where the original details had been modified on the shop floor. *Tornado* is not an exact copy of its forebears; the boiler being a fully welded vessel with steel firebox. Fitted with additional water capacity and the latest railway safety electronics, *Tornado* is fully equipped for today's main line railway.

The £3m needed to build *Tornado* was raised through covenants – an A1 for the price of a pint of beer a week – commercial sponsorship (principal sponsor William Cook Cast Products Ltd), a bearer bond issue and bridging loans. The pace of build was very much dictated by the rate at which the funds could be raised, all the time seeking to overcome the sceptical cries from those who said that it could not – and sometimes should not – be done. Yes, there were some bumps in the road and it certainly took much longer than anticipated but by the spring of 2008 no. 60163 *Tornado* was nearing completion at Darlington Locomotive Works.

**The frames are lifted whilst the crank axle is worked on in October 2002.** Picture by Fastline Photographic courtesy The A1 Steam Locomotive Trust.

**One of the radius rods is forged at John Hesketh & Sons Ltd, Bury, on 25th October 2002.**
Picture by Fastline Photographic courtesy The A1 Steam Locomotive Trust.

**One of the A1 Trust's regular volunteers, Mick Robinson, works on the superheater header, 21st December 2007.**
**Picture by David Elliott courtesy The A1 Steam Locomotive Trust.**

Throughout the existence of The A1 Steam Locomotive Trust, great care has been taken to manage the image of the Trust and of *Tornado*, positioning the locomotive as a great – but slightly quirky – British achievement and I believe that in some part this has helped to change the image of the railway heritage movement over the past few years.

The first fire was lit by Mrs Dorothy Mather, the widow of Arthur Peppercorn then in her 92nd year and President of the Trust and she stated how proud Arthur would have been. The 'media scrum' at *Tornado's* first public move in steam was broadcast live on the BBC and covered as far away as China and Australia.

Following the completion of test and trials on the Great Central Railway, *Tornado* completed three main line trials based out of the National Railway Museum in York during November 2008. The final 75mph test run from York to Newcastle and back was witnessed by thousands from the lineside. However, the phenomena

**The boiler has arrived from Germany and is lifted over the fence at Darlington to be taken into the workshop on 16th July 2006. Photograph by Keith Drury courtesy The A1 Steam Locomotive Trust.**

that is *Tornado* only really hit us on 7th February 2009 with 'The Talisman' from Darlington to London King's Cross. Well-wishers had waved us by all along the southern end of the East Coast Main Line. We entered the trainshed past a huge crowd of people. This was a film star reception! A conservative estimate would be at least 2,000 and most probably a lot more. It has become a defining image of what is now generally referred to as the '*Tornado* effect'.

It was apparent that a significant proportion of the crowd were members of the general public, captivated by the story of success in a shed in Darlington. It was followed just over a week later with the naming of *Tornado* at York railway station by TRH The Prince of Wales and The Duchess of Cornwall.

Of course, *Tornado's* most high profile performance challenge in these early years was the 'Great Race to the North' - the 25th April 2009 London King's Cross to Edinburgh special train for BBC Top Gear. The run was months in the planning by the Trust's Operations Director Graeme Bunker and what resulted was an

**Mick Robinson and Ian Howitt check rod lengths on 19th October 2004.** **Photograph by David Elliott courtesy The A1 Steam Locomotive Trust.**

**Superheater flue tubes are fitted into the boiler in Germany, 4th July 2006.** **Picture by David Elliott courtesy The A1 Steam Locomotive Trust.**

Working on the tender at North View Engineering, Darlington on 29th May 2007. Picture by David Elliott courtesy The A1 Steam Locomotive Trust.

Malcolm Crawley shovels the first coal into the firebox before the lighting of *Tornado's* first fire, 2008. Picture courtesy The A1 Steam Locomotive Trust.

HRH Prince Charles, with the Duchess of Cornwall and Mark Allatt, delivers a speech at the naming ceremony for *Tornado* at York on 19th February 2009. Picture by Neil Whitaker courtesy The A1 Steam Locomotive Trust.

eight-hour, four-stop schedule, representing one of the stiffest performance challenges ever faced in the preservation era. Records tumbled throughout the day as she kept impeccably to her path to achieve the first single-headed ECML end-to-end run by steam since 1968. Actual time on the move was a shade under 6½ hours – an 'Elizabethan' performance! The run ranks alongside the best of ECML performances and the subsequent showing on primetime TV, with the inevitable repeats, has been one of the best bits of publicity for the project to date.

**The cabside number is carefully applied, December 2008.**
**Picture by Malcolm Crawley courtesy The A1 Steam Locomotive Trust.**

*Tornado* has gone on to visit almost every corner of Great Britain, hauling the Royal Train with HRH The Prince of Wales on-board no less than three times, including the first overnight Royal Train for over 50 years from Wembley to Kemble, then up Lickey Incline and on to Bishop Auckland before continuing to Alnmouth and on to Edinburgh. In the early hours of 12th April 2017 *Tornado* became the first British steam locomotive to reach 100mph for 50 years whilst conducting main line tests as part of the approval process to operate at 90mph (as opposed to 75mph) on selected routes.

**No. 60163 *Tornado* heads a passenger train at Kinchley Lane on the Great Central Railway in late September 2008.**
**Photograph by S.J. Taylor courtesy The A1 Steam Locomotive Trust.**

It is down to the Trust's more than 1,000 regular monthly and other donors, sponsors lead by William Cook Cast Products Ltd and the hard work of the Trust's volunteers and contractors that it has got this far. To keep *Tornado* on the main line, the Trust still needs to raise £200,000 to purchase the tender which was kindly paid for by WCCP in 2006 and an estimated £500,000 every five years or so to fund overhauls – the fundraising efforts never stop.

And so, over 50 years since the withdrawal of the last Peppercorn Pacific by British Railways we are incredibly fortunate to have examples of both the class A1s and A2s in existence. *Blue Peter's* preservation career has been one of long periods in the shade but when in the sun the locomotive has been one of the best main line performers. Hopefully it won't be long until we can judge that again for ourselves. There could not have been a more perfect type of locomotive to launch the new build main line steam phenomena than the Peppercorn Class A1. no. 60163 *Tornado* worked 'straight out of the box' when completed in 2008 and has gone on to amaze and delight in equal measure since. Far from being eclipsed by their older Gresley cousins, these two Peppercorn Pacifics are undoubtedly two of the finest steam locomotives ever to operate in Great Britain.

**For details of how to support no. 60163 *Tornado*, or where to see or travel behind her, visit www.a1steam.com, email enquiries@a1steam.com or call 01325 460163.**

***Tornado* takes centre stage in the roundhouse at Barrow Hill's open day, 4th April 2009.**
**Picture by Clive Hanley courtesy The A1 Steam Locomotive Trust.**

On 31st December 1947 a small group of the men responsible for design and construction of London & North Eastern Railway locomotives at Doncaster Works gather to record the completion of the last Pacific locomotive for the company before the formation of British Railways on 1st January 1948. In the centre of the front row is A.H. Peppercorn (with spectacles and hat) the last Chief Mechanical Engineer of the company and designer of the locomotive carrying his name. On his right is J.F. Harrison, Assistant Chief Mechanical Engineer (later Chief Mechanical Engineer of British Railways). B. Spencer, Technical Assistant to Sir Nigel Gresley, is second from the right front row and T. Windle, Chief Draughtsman, is seated on the left of J.F. Harrison.

# INTRODUCTION

The Peppercorn Pacifics were the last great British steam locomotives. The design was the culmination of a long line of noted express engines to be produced at the world-famous Doncaster Works founded by the Great Northern Railway, which was subsequently part of the London & North Eastern Railway. Arthur Henry Peppercorn - the designer of the A1 and A2 Classes - rose through the ranks of the two companies to reach the Chief Mechanical Engineer's chair in 1946. He was then able to couple the best of preceding practice with the demands of the time - simple maintenance and low costs - to great success, although the locomotives remained somewhat overshadowed by their predecessors, the Gresley A3s and A4s.

A.H. Peppercorn.

Born in 1889, Peppercorn, who was one of eleven children sired by Rev. A.T. Peppercorn of Stoke Prior, knew from an early age that he wanted to be involved with railways and after leaving school was taken as a Premium Apprentice at Doncaster Works by H.A. Ivatt during 1905. H.N. Gresley arrived at the same time as Carriage & Wagon Superintendent and the two formed a lifelong friendship.

After completing his apprenticeship, Peppercorn was made Assistant to the Locomotive Inspector at Ardsley but his ability soon saw a promotion granted to Assistant to the Locomotive Superintendent, Peterborough. Following service in the First World War, Peppercorn became District Locomotive Superintendent, Retford, and soon afterwards became Assistant Locomotive Carriage & Wagon Superintendent, Doncaster. In the reorganisation post-Grouping he took the full position at Doncaster, until near the end of the decade he moved to the larger carriage workshops at York in the same role. In the early 1930s Peppercorn become Assistant Mechanical Engineer, Stratford, then in 1937 Locomotive Running Superintendent, Southern Area, and in 1938 Mechanical Engineer, Darlington.

**Peppercorn (looking to camera) during a Royal visit to Doncaster Works on 29th October 1941; Edward Thompson, then CME, is stood in front of him.**

Edward Thompson was slightly senior in years and progressed through the LNER ranks in front of Peppercorn, the former often vacating positions subsequently occupied by the latter. After Gresley's death in 1941, Thompson was appointed CME, with Peppercorn as his Assistant, whilst he also performed the role of Mechanical Engineer, Doncaster. The two men were opposites, both in their view of locomotive design and their demeanours, but this does not appear to have affected their working relationship. Thompson was assisted by Peppercorn up to the former's retirement in 1946.

**Peppercorn (with hat) and group in front of a US Army locomotive at Doncaster Works.**

A standardisation policy had been set in motion by Thompson to improve maintenance and reduce costs during the war years and in doing so left behind a number of Gresley features. Some of these decisions met with success, while others failed for various reasons. When the war was over, Thompson intended to replace the Gresley Pacifics with a new design because these engines had a certain tendency to 'run hot' in the middle big end bearing. The P2 Class 2-8-2s (based on the A3 Class design) were rebuilt in 1944 to prove the intended alterations, including dividing the drive between leading and intermediate axles and using three independent sets of valve gear in place of Gresley's own conjugated motion. This was cited as the cause of the failures - mainly because overwork during the war caused increased wear on the components and reductions in staff numbers caused maintenance standards to fall to unsatisfactory levels.

The case for the changes was proved sufficiently for 30 A2s based on the rebuilds to be authorised in 1944, followed by 13 in 1945. In the event only 15 engines, later classified A2/3, were completed before the design was slightly altered following Peppercorn's succession. The main change was the repositioning of the bogie between the cylinders as the Thompson Pacifics suffered several problems at the front end due to the lack of rigidity in this area. A drawback of the modification here was that the smokebox was shortened because the extra space was no longer necessary, forcing a decision to be made about keeping the self cleaning apparatus or the Kylchap double blastpipe and chimney. Unfortunately for several of the A2s the former was chosen and a single chimney was fitted. There was also a return to the perforated steam collector (also known as the 'banjo' dome) on top of the boiler, which aimed to remove any remaining water from the steam before passing into the superheater, and the v-shaped cab front that reduced glare on the windscreens.

In total 15 A2 locomotives were erected at Doncaster between December 1947 and August 1948, all being named after racehorses, apart from the first which was given *A.H. Peppercorn* to recognise his services to the LNER before the company became defunct. Six of the class were later fitted with Kylchap double blastpipes and chimneys and multiple valve regulators, the latter being an experiment to reduce wear in the superheater. The class was initially predominantly based in England, with only one at Edinburgh Haymarket, before a reorganisation swapped the ex-P2s, which were not well thought of, with the new A2s. In the early 1950s the class were allocated to Aberdeen (3), Dundee (2), Haymarket (6), Gateshead (1), Heaton (1) and York (1); the anomaly was no. 60533 *Happy Knight* which moved several times, but was either at Peterborough or Grantham. In Scotland the class was particularly used on the Edinburgh to Aberdeen services, whilst jaunts into England were made by the Haymarket group, particularly to Carlisle and Newcastle. Those in England were mainly put on secondary expresses and freight services.

**An A2 boiler in the hydraulic riveter at Doncaster on 19th November 1947.**

Peppercorn also took over Thompson's plans for a Pacific with 6 ft 8 in. diameter wheels and similarly modified them, borrowing much from the A2 rather than the rebuild of Gresley A1 no. 4470 *Great Northern*. Many of the changes made from the former design were minor and necessary because of the larger coupled wheels, whilst the most important divergence was the fitting of Kylchap double blastpipes and chimneys from new which improved the steaming and efficiency of the locomotives. Sixteen were ordered initially, followed by twenty-three from Darlington and then 10 more from Doncaster after Nationalisation. All were in traffic by December 1949 and were stabled at most of the major sheds of the former LNER, working many of the main express trains, taking over from Gresley A3s and V2s.

Forging the connecting rod of an A2 Class engine.

The first A2 Class Pacific - no. 525 - comes together in the New Erecting Shop at Doncaster as the frames are mated with the boiler on 26th November 1947.

**An A2 - perhaps no. 527 *Sun Chariot* - is wheeled in the New Erecting Shop on 15th January 1948.**

Peppercorn had retired by the time his last Pacific - no. 60162 *Saint Johnstoun* - entered service and in the 13 months that followed up to his death on 3rd March 1951 he perhaps heard reports as to how well they were performing. Unfortunately, he would not be told how reliable they would prove, averaging over 100,000 miles between general repairs - five were fitted with Timken roller bearings on all axles and some of these engines ran a lot further without works attention - when earlier LNER Pacifics only achieved average mileages of 80,000. In comparison with express locomotives from other regions of BR, the A1 Pacifics were found to be very economical with regard maintenance costs.

In the early 1950s the A1s at King's Cross shed were swapped with A4s from other depots to rationalise maintenance and stores of parts for the two classes. Gateshead held the largest stud at 14, with Grantham and Leeds Copley Hill joint second with 10, followed by York, Heaton, Edinburgh Haymarket and Ardsley. Many of the main line expresses were worked in sections at this time, with Grantham and Newcastle being the main points for engine changes. After the middle of the decade had passed another reorganisation was implemented and King's Cross regained a number of A1s so trains could be taken from there to Newcastle without switching locomotives. Throughout the 1950s the A1s were averaging over 200 miles per day and some even more.

Such results were too late in the day for steam locomotives as the Modernisation Plan, formulated by BR to improve the network and services offered, decreed that diesel locomotives were to be introduced. This occurred in an ever increasing rate from the late 1950s and from the end of 1962 the Peppercorn Pacifics began to be withdrawn. Many were only halfway through their expected lifespan and as the 1960s progressed more were sent to the scrap yard. Opportunities to save locomotives were very limited and

No. 525 in the Paint Shop, Doncaster.

difficult to realise. At the last minute no. 60532 *Blue Peter* was bought privately though all 49 A1s were lost.

The A2 did not run for a prolonged period until the 1990s after a full overhaul was carried out. At the same time a group came together to form the A1 Steam Locomotive Trust with the aim of building a new A1 Pacific. This pioneering project was subsequently embraced and, following 15 years of hard work, no. 60163 *Tornado* was completed in 2008, re-establishing the legacy of the class for present and future generations.

J.F. Harrison presents A.H. Peppercorn with a small radio and radiogram, which had been subscribed for by friends and colleagues, both past and present, for his retirement on 31st December 1949.

*Above*
No. 60114 at the south end of Gas Works Tunnel, King's Cross station. The locomotive was allocated to King's Cross shed from new in early August 1948 and remained employed at the depot until June 1950.

*Below*
In the climate of post-war austerity, naming locomotives was not deemed a priority, though no. 60114 was given the honour in October 1948. W.P. Allen had just been appointed to the Railway Executive to handle matters relating to the workforce; he had previously been employed as General Secretary for ASLEF.

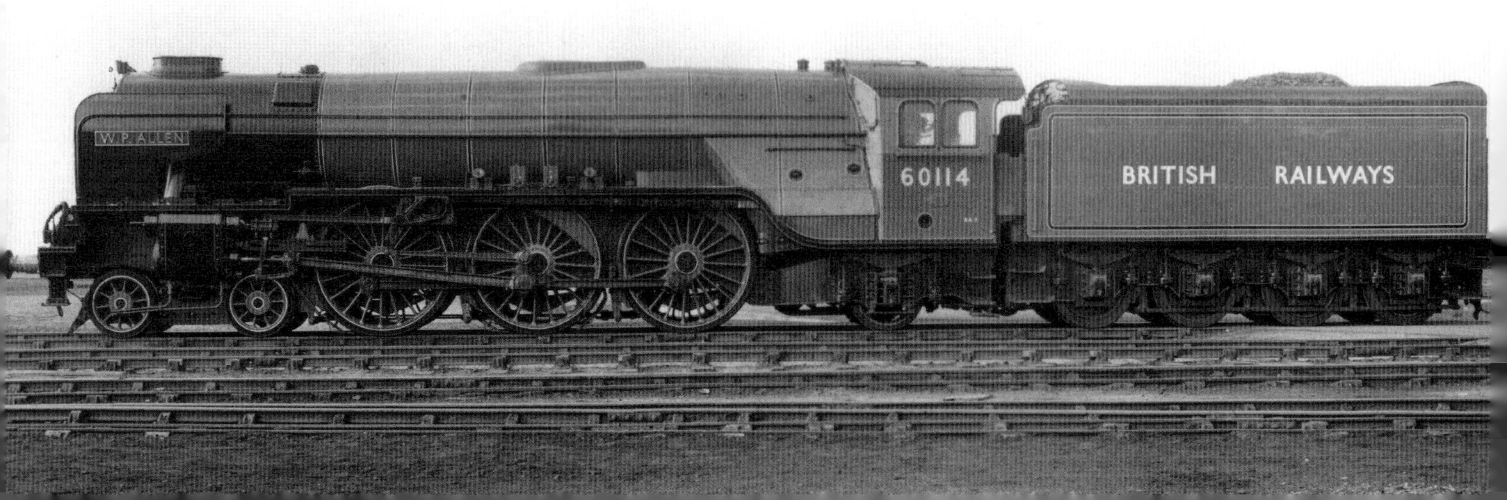

*Above*
At the head of the Gainsborough Model Railway Society's excursion to Blackpool from Lincoln on 28th September 1963 is no. 60114. Photographed at Doncaster by Geoff Warnes.

*Below*
No. 60114 *W.P. Allen* was allocated to Doncaster shed (visible in the background from the south end) in September 1957 and is seen there a year later. Picture by Bill Reed.

*Above*
An arrival at King's Cross station has blocked the view of a large number of 'spotters' camped at the end of the platform as no. 60114 prepares to depart with 'The West Riding'; Gresley N2 no. 69584 is also present.

*Below*
Heading north on the west side of York station (past the goods sidings on the right) with a parcels train is no. 60114 on 25th June 1964; the engine would be withdrawn by the end of the year. Picture by B.W.L. Brooksbank.

*Above*
No. 60115 *Meg Merrilies* heads north through Belle Isle with the 15.10 express from King's Cross to Newcastle on 1st July 1958. Picture by P.N. Townend.

*Below*
Beginning the long journey to King's Cross from Edinburgh Waverley station with the 'Flying Scotsman' is no. 60115. Picture by Eric Treacy courtesy David Joy.

*Above*
Gateshead-based *Meg Merrilies* stands ready for departure at Edinburgh Waverley on 11th April 1957. Picture by Bill Reed.

*Below*
The fireman of no. 60115 has a minute in his seat before toiling with the shovel upon leaving Newcastle Central station. Photograph by D.J. Dippie.

*Above*
Another view of no. 60115 at Newcastle on 13th February 1960. Picture by D.J. Dippie.

*Below*
*Meg Merrilies* is serviced at Edinburgh Haymarket shed around 1958. The locomotive left Gateshead shed at the end of 1960 and transferred to Leeds Copley Hill. Picture by Bill Reed.

*Hal o' the Wynd* and *Meg Merrilies* at Edinburgh Haymarket. Photograph by Bill Reed.

*Above*
No. 60116 - fresh from the first general repair, which was carried out between January and March 1950 - is seen outside the Paint Shop at Doncaster Works. Picture by Malcolm Crawley.

*Below*
No. 60116 travels north through Monkwearmouth station on 15th May 1961. The locomotive had been allocated to Heaton from new in October 1948. Photograph by D.J. Dippie.

60116
HAL O' THE WYND
60116

60116

*Above*
View south from above Copenhagen Tunnel, King's Cross, as no. 60117 *Bois Roussel* approaches with an express to Leeds and Bradford. The train is passing under the bridge carrying the North London line between Caledonian Road and Maiden Lane stations. The central span of the bridge frames the lines to the goods sidings, engine shed and goods station. Picture by Eric Treacy courtesy David Joy.

*Opposite above*
After being prepared to work the down 'Queen of Scots Pullman' service, *Hal o' the Wynd* has been captured running back to Leeds Central station. Picture courtesy *Yorkshire Post Newspapers.*

*Opposite below*
No. 60116 eases out of the north end of York station with the down 'Heart of Midlothian'. The train was timed to depart King's Cross at 13.15, York 17.30 for arrival in Edinburgh at 20.30. Photograph by Eric Treacy courtesy David Joy.

*Above*
Three generations of LNER Pacifics stand outside King's Cross locomotive shed on 1st August 1959. No. 60108 *Gay Crusader* was the eighth Gresley A1 Pacific to be erected at Doncaster and was later rebuilt there to A3 specifications. No. 60033 *Seagull* was the penultimate A4 built in 1938 and was fitted from new with a Kylchap double blastpipe and chimney which made the engine one of the better class members. No. 60117 entered traffic in October 1948 and was allocated to Copley Hill shed at this time. Picture by P.N. Townend.

*Below*
No. 60117's 5,000 gallon tender is replenished at Muskham water troughs, just north of Newark, on 2nd June 1956. Photograph by Bill Reed.

*Above*
No. 60118 looks quite dishevelled at the head of an unidentified express at King's Cross station.

*Below*
No. 60118 *Archibald Sturrock* has been stopped by a signal at Copley Hill, Leeds, whilst heading to Leeds Central station with the 'Queen of Scots' Pullman on 1st August 1952. Picture courtesy *Yorkshire Post Newspapers*.

Copley Hill's *Archibald Sturrock* stands on the west side of Grantham station on tracks that were part of the locomotive depot. The mechanical coaler - with a 200-ton capacity - was erected around 1937/1938 by Henry Lees & Co., replacing the old coal stage, which was retained for emergencies/busy periods and located behind the engine on the north side of the coaler. Given the level the fireman is standing, the remaining coal in the tender is perhaps being packed in before further supplies are obtained. Picture by Bill Reed.

No. 60118 is again seen in the Copley Hill area, but on this occasion - 2nd August 1952 - *Archibald Sturrock* is light engine and waiting for a B1 with the Bristol train to clear the tracks. Photograph courtesy *Yorkshire Post Newspapers*.

A short time later and *Archibald Sturrock* has collected the 'Yorkshire Pullman' from Leeds Central and is just entering Holbeck station at the start of the journey south to King's Cross. Picture courtesy *Yorkshire Post Newspapers*.

*Above*
No. 60119 *Patrick Stirling* at the end of the platform at Grantham with a train heading north on 24th May 1962. Picture by Cedric Clayson courtesy The A1 Steam Locomotive Trust.

*Below*
Doncaster-allocated no. 60119 arrives at Grantham station with a down express on 12th September 1958. The engine had been recently transferred from King's Cross shed after a year there. Picture by Bill Reed.

*Above*
No. 60119 on the outskirts of Leeds with the 'Queen of Scots' Pullman. Picture courtesy *Yorkshire Post Newspapers*.

*Below*
*Patrick Stirling* at Doncaster shed, September 1958. Picture by Bill Reed.

No. 60120 *Kittiwake* approaches Grantham with a down express on 1st June 1962, passing a DMU stopped by a signal in the process. Picture by Cedric Clayson courtesy The A1 Steam Locomotive Trust.

*Above*
Another year would elapse before King's Cross-allocated no. 60120 received nameplates. The engine is seen at Potters Bar in May 1949 with the 15.30 train to Newcastle.
*Below*
By June 1950 *Kittiwake* had been sent north to Copley Hill shed and the locomotive is seen near there at Wortley South Junction on 17th March 1951. Picture courtesy *Yorkshire Post Newspapers*.

60121
SILURIAN
60121

*Opposite above*

York's no. 60121 *Silurian* heads a train of empty coaching stock out of the south end of Sunderland station on 6th June 1962. Picture by D.J. Dippie.

*Opposite below*

From being sent into traffic in late December 1948 until withdrawal in early October 1965, no. 60121 was allocated to York shed. The engine is perhaps pictured in sidings to the west of the main building (also the station) as the carriages seen in the background were stabled adjacent to the locomotives. Photograph by Bill Reed.

*Below*

An interesting view of *Silurian* - and a trestle wagon loaded with metal plates - in Portobello Lane goods sidings, Monkwearmouth, Sunderland, on 24th December 1960. The engine had accumulated plenty of dirt and grime since entering traffic after a general repair in January and had probably received the AWS apparatus at this time; the connection between the apparatus at the front of the locomotive and the cab is seen attached to the edge of the running plate. Picture by D.J. Dippie.

*Above*
No. 60121 with a down express at Alnmouth in September 1964; note the large amount of steam leaking from the rear of the first coach. Picture by Bill Reed.

*Below*
*Silurian* at the north end of Monkwearmouth station with a goods train on 15th July 1960. Picture by D.J. Dippie.

*Above*
No. 60122 exits the north end of Hadley Wood North Tunnel with the down 'White Rose' express in 1949.

*Below*
No. 60122 *Curlew* (named July 1950) is cleaned at Grantham shed between 1951 and 1952 when in residence there.

For the final few years in service no. 60122 *Curlew* was allocated to Doncaster shed and the locomotive is seen there around 1960 with Gresley O2 Class 2-8-0 no. 63973. Despite being the younger of the two, *Curlew* was scrapped in 1962, whilst no. 63973 survived for another year. Photograph by Bill Reed.

*Above*
No. 60122 light engine at the south end of Grantham station in June 1958. Picture by Bill Reed.

*Below*
No. 60122 is still nameless despite having the first BR emblem on the tender. The latter addition was made on 20th July 1950, the plates being cast on 7th March 1950. The engine is seen south of York with an Edinburgh to King's Cross express. Picture by Eric Treacy courtesy David Joy.

H.A.IVATT
60123

60123
H.A.IVATT

*Above*
After undergoing non-classified repairs in late September 1958, no. 60123 is seen at Doncaster shed ready to return to traffic. Photograph by Bill Reed.

*Opposite above*
No. 60123 *H.A. Ivatt* at Leeds Central station on 17th October 1951; the locomotive had only just been transferred from Copley Hill to Ardsley shed. Picture courtesy *Yorkshire Post Newspapers*.

*Opposite below*
On 7th September 1962 no. 60123 was derailed near Offord whilst working the King's Cross to Leeds freight service, causing the extensive damage seen here. As a result the locomotive was withdrawn on 1st October and scrapped at Doncaster. Picture courtesy Richard Postill.

*Above*
Passing over Werrington water troughs, just north of Peterborough, is no. 60124 *Kenilworth* which is attached to the 'Flying Scotsman' express. The troughs were nearly 550 metres long and could fill the tender with 2,000 gallons in 20 seconds when travelling around 60 mph.

*Below*
Seen at York with an express on 18th September 1965 no. 60124 *Kenilworth* still had six months to go before withdrawal, but the nameplates and worksplates have already been removed to stop those not willing to pay for their trophy. Photograph by Bill Reed.

Minus cab in the Crimpsall Repair Shop, Doncaster, no. 60124 was undergoing non-classified attention when pictured on 17th September 1961. The engine spent a month in works from 29th August to September and in the meantime had been reallocated to York from Heaton. Picture by Cedric Clayson courtesy The A1 Steam Locomotive Trust.

*Kenilworth* on the turntable at Edinburgh Haymarket, 2nd July 1961. Photograph by Bill Reed.

60124

*Above*
No. 60125 *Scottish Union* at platform five, King's Cross station, with B1 no. 61179 at the head of an express from Grimsby, which has just arrived on 29th December 1960. Photograph by B.W.L. Brooksbank.

*Opposite above*
Late in 1965 no. 60124 stands near the turntable at Darlington shed on standby duty in case any of the new diesels should fail and the train require assistance. Picture by D.J. Dippie.

*Opposite below*
*Kenilworth* heads north from Monkwearmouth station on 30th June 1961; a diesel locomotive can be seen on the right in the goods yard. Photograph by D.J. Dippie.

*Above*
Grantham's no. 60125 departs King's Cross with an express for York around 1955. Picture by Eric Treacy courtesy David Joy.

*Below*
*Scottish Union* (named after the winning racehorse of the 1938 St Leger) waits at Doncaster shed to be called into works for a general repair in late September 1958. Photograph by Bill Reed.

*Above*
No. 60125 makes a nice display for the camera upon departure from Leeds Central station with an express on 2nd August 1952. Picture courtesy *Yorkshire Post Newspapers*.

*Below*
Seen on the ash pits at Grantham shed in mid-1957, *Scottish Union* was coming to the end of the allocation there and would soon move on to King's Cross. Picture by Bill Reed.

60126
BRITISH RAILWAYS
60126
60126
SIR VINCENT
60126

*Above*
No. 60126 passes through Heaton cutting, Newcastle, with empty stock at 12.00 on 24th May 1961. Photograph by D.J. Dippie.

*Opposite above*
The last A1 to enter traffic with LNER apple green livery was no. 60126 which stands outside the Weigh House at Doncaster shortly before entering service in April 1949. Picture by P.N. Townend.

*Opposite below*
Heaton's no. 60126 *Sir Vincent Raven* at Neville Hill shed, Leeds, between duties on 27th November 1951. Photograph courtesy *Yorkshire Post Newspapers*.

No. 60126 was named after the last CME of the North Eastern Railway in August 1950 and was appropriately allocated to sheds with strong connections to the old company - Heaton and York. The locomotive is seen on former GNR territory at Doncaster shed around 1960. Photograph by Bill Reed.

Another former CME of the NER had the honour of having an A1 carry his name as no. 60127 became *Wilson Worsdell* from September 1950. The engine is seen loitering on the west side of Doncaster station on 14th July 1957. Picture by Bill Reed.

Heaton-based no. 60127 heads an express at Monkwearmouth on 2nd July 1960. Picture by D.J. Dippie.

60127

60127
34

*Above*
From October 1964 to withdrawal in June 1965 no. 60127 was allocated to Gateshead shed, where the engine is seen in early 1965. Photograph by Bill Reed.

*Opposite above*
Leaving York with a train bound for Newcastle is no. 60127. Picture by Eric Treacy courtesy David Joy.

*Opposite below*
*Wilson Worsdell* at Durham on 16th July 1960 with a down express. The engine is passing Durham locomotive shed on the right. Picture by D.J. Dippie.

60128
BONGRACE

*Above*
No. 60128 is seen with the 'West Riding' express and the image dates to early July 1949; the locomotive was only two months old and was sent into traffic wearing the new BR blue colour scheme. King's Cross station provides the backdrop.

*Opposite above*
No. 60128 *Bongrace* is attached to an up express at Grantham station during June 1958. The locomotive was allocated to King's Cross shed at this time. Picture by Bill Reed.

*Opposite below*
No. 60128 was 16 months away from being named when photographed with the northbound 'West Riding' express at Potters Bar on 17th July 1949. The engine was Copley Hill-based at this time.

*Page 58 above*
Leaving York with the down 'Flying Scotsman' is no. 60128 *Bongrace*. The engine has Grantham's 35B shedcode on the smokebox door and this was in place between September 1951 and September 1957. Picture by Eric Treacy courtesy David Joy.

*Page 58 below*
Another view of *Bongrace* at York but in this instance the location is the locomotive shed, where water is being filled into the tender. The 34A shedplate denotes King's Cross where the engine was based from June 1950 to September 1951. Photograph by Eric Treacy courtesy David Joy.

60128

60128
BONGRACE
60128
0976

*Above*
No. 60129 *Guy Mannering* at York. The locomotive was briefly allocated there for three months after construction on June 1949. Picture by Eric Treacy courtesy David Joy.

*Below*
Footplatemen pose with *Guy Mannering* at Edinburgh Haymarket shed before leaving for Waverley station. After leaving York, no. 60129 settled at Gateshead and spent 11 years there until 1960 when moving to Tweedmouth.

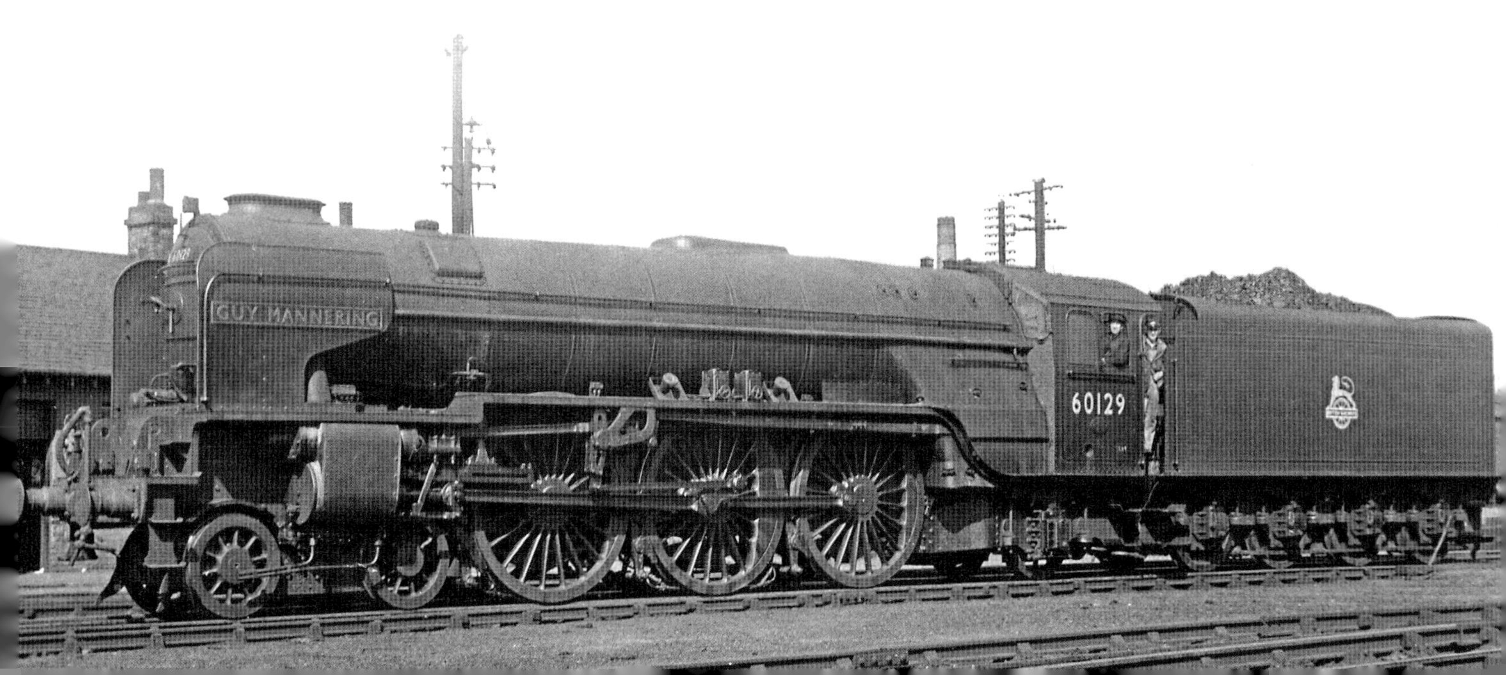

60129

60129

*Above*
The 07.53 express to King's Cross leaves Sunderland station behind no. 60129 on 15th June 1961. Photograph by D.J. Dippie.

*Opposite above*
No. 60129 glides under the main road bridge, which has since been replaced, at Croxdale on 12th June 1954. Picture by B.W.L. Brooksbank.

*Opposite below*
*Guy Mannering* heads north out of York with a modest train of Gresley compartment carriages. Photograph by Eric Treacy courtesy David Joy.

No. 60130 *Kestrel* on the main line near Bawtry with the 'Harrogate Sunday Pullman' on 14th July 1957. At this time the engine was employed by Ardsley shed, but would soon be transferred to Copley Hill. Picture by Bill Reed.

No. 60130 with an express at Great Ponton, south of Grantham, 13th April 1962. Photograph by Bill Reed.

Official picture of *Kestrel* taken at Doncaster Works after the engine's last general repair which was completed during the first six weeks of 1963. The locomotive would continue in traffic for a further two years and eight months.

*Above*
The finishing touches are applied to no. 60130 in Darlington Works Paint Shop shortly before the locomotive entered traffic at the end of September 1948. Picture courtesy J.W. Armstrong Trust.

*Page 67 above*
In mid-December 1964 *Osprey* was admitted to Darlington Works for the first time since construction and underwent three-weeks' worth of attention following more than two years in traffic. At the end of January 1965 the locomotive was back for another six weeks in the Repair Shop and no. 60131 is seen here close to the end on 27th February 1965 with A4 no. 60019 *Bittern* and Worsdell J27 no. 65804. Picture by N.W. Skinner, courtesy J.W. Armstrong Trust.

*Page 67 below*
In the process of connecting to the 13.15 from King's Cross to Harrogate during March 1955 is no. 60131 *Osprey*.

*Above*
Wiske Moor water troughs, south of Darlington, quench the thirst of no. 60131 *Osprey* which is at the head of the 'Flying Scotsman' on 1st August 1951.

*Below*
*Osprey* at Great Ponton on 8th May 1960. Picture by Bill Reed.

No. 60131 entered traffic from Darlington in October 1948 and was subsequently named in June 1950. The engine is seen at King's Cross c. 1960. Photograph by Bill Reed.

65804
OSPREY

60131

*Above*
No. 60132 *Marmion* hurries north with the 09.30 from King's Cross to Newcastle on 21st April 1951. The locomotive had been named less than six months and was Gateshead-allocated from new in October 1948 to May 1960.

*Below*
Now working from Tweedmouth, *Marmion* is serviced at Edinburgh Haymarket shed during July 1963. The engine returned to Gateshead at the end of 1964 for six months before withdrawal. Picture by D.J. Dippie.

*Above*
An interesting shot of no. 60132's coupled wheels in the Crimpsall Repair Shop, Doncaster, as a general repair comes to an end on 17th September 1961. Picture by Cedric Clayson, courtesy The A1 Steam Locomotive Trust.

*Below*
No. 60132 gets away from York with a down express for Newcastle. Picture by D.J. Dippie.

*Above*
No. 60133 *Pommern* with the 'North Briton' headboard. The service between Leeds, York, Edinburgh and Glasgow began in the early 20th century and lasted until the late 1970s.

*Opposite below*
*Pommern* receives coal from the stage at Copley Hill; the locomotive was allocated to the shed from 1950 to 1964. Photograph by Eric Treacy courtesy David Joy.

*Above*
No. 60133 runs backwards into the Gasworks Tunnel, passing two suburban tanks (69495 and 69583) heading north on 1st August 1958. Picture by P.N. Townend.

*Above*
No. 60134 on the turntable at King's Cross station locomotive yard, c. 1950. The engine is decorated in LNER apple green livery and has an irregular lining applied to the tender.

*Opposite*
Two views of no. 60133 passing Great Ponton - two miles from Stoke summit and three miles from Grantham - on 8th May 1960. Photograph by Bill Reed.

*Below*
Copley Hill's no. 60134 heads the down 'Yorkshire Pullman' at New Southgate on 9th April 1949.

Three views of no. 60134 *Foxhunter* at Grantham - two at the station, one at the shed - as the engine is removed from the 'BR Bulb Fields' excursion after arrival from York and then serviced. The locomotive was sent into traffic from Darlington in August 1948, then named in October 1950 after the winner of the Doncaster Cup in 1932. All photographs by Bill Reed.

BULB FIELDS
EXCURSION
FOXHUNTER

BULB FIELDS
EXCURSION
FOXHUNTER
60134

*Above*
No. 60134 *Foxhunter* takes a brief breath of fresh air after exiting the 1,046 yard-long Welwyn North tunnel before entering the 446-yard Welwyn South tunnel. The locomotive is at the head of the up 'Yorkshire Pullman'.

*Below*
Reversing out to Copley Hill after working a train into Leeds Central station on 22nd November 1951 is no. 60134 *Foxhunter*. After leaving the aforementioned shed in April 1962, the engine had spells at Ardsley and Neville Hill before withdrawal in October 1965. Photograph courtesy *Yorkshire Post Newspapers*.

*Opposite*
A front end study of no. 60135, which appears to have recently entered traffic - from Darlington in November 1948. Pictured at York, the engine was allocated to Gateshead from new and was based there until 1960.

60135
L
T
A1.

*Above*
No. 60135 *Madge Wildfire* rushes through Durham station with an express on 16th July 1960. Changes from the previous picture of the locomotive include the addition of a lip to the chimney, repositioning of the smokebox number plate, AWS fitted to the bufferbeam and nameplates (October 1950). The engine would be taken into Doncaster Works for the last general repair at the start of August and another two years would be spent at work, first from Copley Hill, then Ardsley. In November 1962 *Madge Wildfire* was condemned and later scrapped at Doncaster. Picture by D.J. Dippie.

*Below*
No. 60135 crosses the swing bridge at Selby with an Edinburgh to King's Cross express during October 1951. Trains running between the two places took a route further west via Knottingley until the NER shortened the distance from York to Doncaster by laying a new line by way of Selby. The Hull & Selby Railway had already installed a bascule bridge to cross the River Ouse, but as time progressed this became inadequate and a swing bridge was installed during the 1890s.

*Above*
The driver of no. 60136 *Alcazar* proudly poses with his steed in between the task of checking and oiling the various motion components. Caught at Copley Hill shed, the Grantham-based engine previously resided at the depot from leaving Darlington at the end of November 1948 until May 1950. Photograph courtesy *Yorkshire Post Newspapers*.

*Below*
During the Christmas and New Year period of 1955 and 1956 no. 60136 was in Doncaster Works for a general repair. Before heading back into traffic, *Alcazar* posed for the works photographer on 13th January 1956.

*Above*

Another view of no. 60136 *Alcazar* at Doncaster Works that is most likely to have been taken in December 1950 when named and newly painted blue; this livery only lasted 13 months. Only maintained by Doncaster, the locomotive visited there a total of 23 times during 14 years and six months in traffic. There were a total of eight general repairs over the years, the remainder being for minor matters. Picture by Malcolm Crawley.

*Below*
No. 60136 *Alcazar* heads towards Grantham with a down express. The locomotive was named in December 1950 after the winner of the Doncaster Gold Cup in 1934. Picture by Bill Reed.

*Above*
Grantham's no. 60136 *Alcazar* is seen at York with the early afternoon express to King's Cross. Several changes of allocation occurred during the locomotive's time in traffic. After leaving Darlington Works in late November 1948 *Alcazar* began work from Copley Hill, but six months later moved on to King's Cross. At the end of the summer season the following year no. 60136 moved north to Grantham for the engine's longest spell at a depot - six years seven months - then spending brief periods at King's Cross, Doncaster and King's Cross before returning to Doncaster in April 1959 and was withdrawn from there in May 1963 and scrapped at the works. Photograph by Eric Treacy courtesy David Joy.

60137

*Above*
No. 60137 *Redgauntlet* at the head of an up express to King's Cross at Durham in late summer 1960. Most of the summer season had been missed by the locomotive as a general repair had been undertaken at Doncaster, but was in traffic again by the time of the August bank holiday. Whilst in works the engine received a fresh boiler - no. 29846 which had previously been with no. 60123 *H.A. Ivatt*, 60535 *Hornets Beauty*, 60136 *Alcazar* and no. 60162 *Saint Johnstoun* when new (as boiler no. 10599).

*Opposite*
View westward through Princes Street Gardens as no. 60137 *Redgauntlet* approaches Edinburgh Waverley station with an express from Glasgow bound for Newcastle during the late 1950s. The spire on the right belongs to the Parish Church of St Cuthbert and the long, imposing building in the background is the Caledonian Hotel, which was erected at the turn of the century for travellers using Edinburgh's other mainline station - Princes Street.

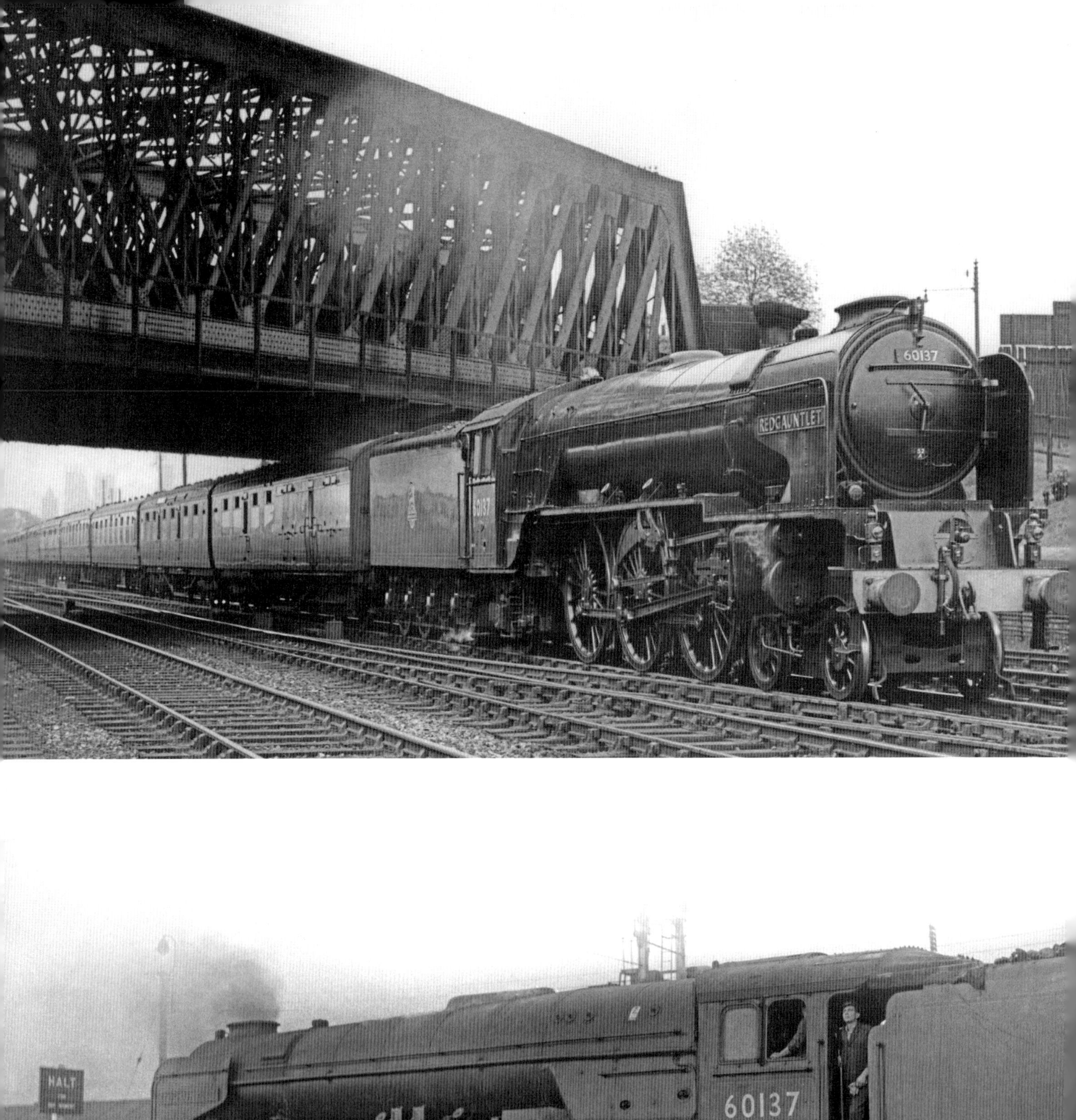
60137
REDGAUNTLET

HALT
60137

*Above*
No. 60138 *Boswell* and no. 60157 *Great Eastern* (obscured on the right) outside the Weigh House at Doncaster Works in early 1962. During the course of the respective general repairs, which took place over the Christmas period, the locomotives both had their top lamp irons lowered and split handrails fitted.

*Opposite above*
Next stop Doncaster for no. 60137 *Redgauntlet* which is heading the up 'Heart Of Midlothian' out of York station on 20th May 1953. Along with Peterborough, the town was not called at during the down service. Photograph by Eric Treacy courtesy David Joy.

*Opposite below*
*Redgauntlet* stands in the yard at Grantham shed - opposite the station - during preparations for working the next train during May 1960. Picture by Bill Reed.

*Above*
Approaching Doncaster from the north with an up train of hopper wagons is no. 60138 *Boswell* on 10th April 1965. Picture by Roger Bastin courtesy The A1 Steam Locomotive Trust.

*Below*
York shed's lifetime resident *Boswell* is attached to goods vans in Portobello Lane goods yard, Sunderland, on 12th April 1963. Interestingly, the engine was one of only three class members based solely at one depot, which in all three cases was York. Photograph by D.J. Dippie.

*Above*
Entering traffic from Darlington in December 1948, no. 60138 *Boswell* was in service for 17 years before being condemned for scrap. The engine is seen at Newcastle on 11th June 1960. Picture by D.J. Dippie.

*Below*
No. 60138 approaches Selby from the north on 10th April 1965. Picture by Roger Bastin courtesy The A1 Steam Locomotive Trust.

YORKSHIRE
PULLMAN
60139
BRITISH RAILWAYS
60139

60139
65

*Above*
Two of Copley Hill's resident A1s - no. 60139 *Sea Eagle* and no. 60141 *Abbotsford* - are seen at the depot in between duties on 2nd August 1952. Gresley J50 0-6-0T no. 68911 and an unidentified 0-6-0 are also present. Photograph courtesy *Yorkshire Post Newspapers*.

*Opposite above*
No. 60139 at King's Cross before departure with the 'Yorkshire Pullman', perhaps during 1949; the locomotive entered traffic just before Christmas 1948.

*Opposite below*
Named *Sea Eagle* in May 1950, no. 60139 heads south away from Retford with an express on 20th August 1958. Photograph by Bill Reed.

*Page 93 above*
Within the confines of Gasworks Tunnel, King's Cross, the driver's side sight screen has become dirty and receives a clean as no. 60139 progresses northward with the down 'Tees-Tyne Pullman' on 31st May 1957. Picture by P.N. Townend.

*Page 93 below*
*Sea Eagle* at York with a northbound express on 13th August 1962. Picture courtesy Richard Postill.

Just south of Grantham station is no. 60139 *Sea Eagle*. After spells at King's Cross and Copley Hill sheds, the engine was allocated to Grantham from December 1955 to April 1957. *Sea Eagle* is seen here in the early 1960s when a Doncaster locomotive, having moved from King's Cross in April 1959 after almost exactly two years there. Picture by Bill Reed.

TEES-TYNE PULLMAN
60139
SEA EAGLE
60139

60139
A1

*Below*
No. 60146 *Balmoral* entered traffic from Darlington Works in late December 1948 and was briefly allocated to York shed from new until October 1949. Eight years later (13th April) the locomotive is seen at the depot under preparation for working a service and is about to receive water, with the fireman just getting on top of the tender and the driver at the water cock. Photograph by Bill Reed.

*Opposite above*
View from the south end of Sunderland station as no. 60140 *Balmoral* departs with an up express on 27th March 1960. The locomotive had relatively recently returned to work after a general overhaul and would continue in service for almost two and a half years before the final visit to Doncaster Works, although an intermediate repair was carried out in the middle of this period. Picture by D.J. Dippie.

*Opposite below*
Coming off the viaduct on the southern approach to Durham station on 15th July 1961 is no. 60140. Leaving King's Cross shed to return to York in June 1950 the engine remained allocated there through to withdrawal in January 1965. Photograph by D.J. Dippie.

60140
B4

60140

60141

60141

*Above*
No. 60141 adjacent to King's Cross station signal box which was opened in October 1932 and survived to September 1971 when replaced by a power signal box. This event was some way off when *Abbotsford* was captured at the head of this mid-afternoon express on 13th October 1950.

*Opposite above*
At Grantham station with an unidentified up Pullman service on 12th September 1958 is no. 60141 *Abbotsford*. Photograph by Bill Reed.

*Opposite below*
Just north of Hatfield station no. 60141 *Abbotsford* thunders forwards with a down express on 22nd August 1960. Picture by D.J. Dippie.

*Page 99 above*
No. 60142 *Edward Fletcher* makes an event of starting off with an unidentified express at Edinburgh Waverley station during the early 1950s.

*Page 99 below*
Fifty-four miles south of Edinburgh and no. 60142 *Edward Fletcher* passes the marker for the border between England and Scotland with an up express. At one time only one sign was present on the up side of the line, which followed the coastline between Berwick and Burnmouth (approx. five miles) and when travelling south fell at a gradient of 1 in 190, but subsequently a second post was installed for passengers travelling north to track their progress.

Driver and fireman of no. 60141 *Abbotsford*, along with shed staff at Copley Hill, Leeds, happily pose in the yard on 1st August 1952. The engine was based at the depot from May 1950 (having left King's Cross after six months there) to September 1963 when heading east to York, where no. 60141 had originally been allocated. *Abbotsford* was condemned there in October 1964. Photograph courtesy *Yorkshire Post Newspapers*.

60142

B.R.
SCOTLAND
60142

EDWARD FLETCHER

60142
EDWARD FLETCHER
60142

*Above*
Seen just north of Monkwearmouth station, Sunderland, is Heaton's no. 60143 *Sir Walter Scott* with a down express for Newcastle on 15th June 1961. Picture by D.J. Dippie.

*Opposite above*
Built at Darlington in February 1949 no. 60142 *Edward Fletcher* and was allocated to Gateshead shed. The locomotive is seen at Newcastle Central station on 11th June 1960 shortly before a move to Heaton occurred. Picture by D.J. Dippie.

*Opposite below*
As *Edward Fletcher* was based in the north east until withdrawal in June 1965, the locomotive would have been very familiar with Edinburgh Haymarket shed's turntable, which moves the locomotive here on 11th April 1957. After two years at Heaton another two were spent at Tweedmouth before returning to Gateshead. Photograph by Bill Reed.

*Below*
Before heading back to the fray no. 60143 *Sir Walter Scott* is photographed at Doncaster Works after undergoing a general repair which lasted from 10th August to 15th September 1950. During this time the engine received the name of the famous Scottish novelist and was given BR's blue livery in place of LNER apple green. The engine had been in traffic since February 1949 and this was the third visit to Doncaster after two previous stays for light attention.

*Opposite*
Water troughs were a relatively late addition to the GNR main line as two sets were not provided until 1900. One of these was Werrington, whilst the other was Muskham (over 700 yards in length) where no. 60143 is seen making use of the vital facility for long-distance expresses. Photograph by Bill Reed.

*Page 105 above*
No. 60144 *King's Courier* has a fresh load of coal on the fire, which does nothing to improve the air quality, as the engine gets away from York with the up 'Heart of Midlothian' during the early 1950s. Photograph by Eric Treacy courtesy David Joy.

*Page 105 below*
North of York with an express for Edinburgh is *King's Courier*. Picture courtesy *Yorkshire Post Newspapers*.

60143

60143

No. 60144 *King's Courier* takes on water at the south end of Doncaster shed in the late 1950s. The locomotive was first allocated to the depot after being completed at Darlington at the beginning of March 1949, although by the end of the year a move away had been engineered. The second spell began in November 1957. Picture by Bill Reed.

60144

60144

No. 60144 visits Doncaster Works with unidentified classmate for attention during the mid- to late 1950s. A total of 17 visits were made to the works over the course of the locomotive's career, which came to an end in April 1963 and *King's Courier* was dismantled there. Photograph by Bill Reed.

*Left*
An atmospheric study of *King's Courier* captured at the north end of platform five, Grantham station, as the locomotive waits to continue northward with a fully fitted freight on 18th April 1963. Picture by Cedric Clayson courtesy The A1 Steam Locomotive Trust.

*Below*
The driver of no. 60144 smiles for the camera before heading north with an express out of King's Cross, c. 1955. The locomotive was allocated to King's Cross depot for two short spells during 14 years in traffic and also worked from Copley Hill, Ardsley and Grantham.

*Above*
Fifteen years after being completed at Darlington in 1949, no. 60145 *Saint Mungo* is back at the works for the first time and undergoes light attention which would keep the engine in traffic until condemned. Picture by Malcolm Dunnett courtesy J.W. Armstrong Trust.

*Below*
On 19th March 1966 no. 60145 - seen at York - had only eight days left in service before being withdrawn. However, three weeks later the locomotive was given a reprieve for two months. Picture by Geoff Warnes.

*Above*
*Saint Mungo* had the honour of working the last official steam express from Newcastle to York and back on 31st December 1965. Seen in the cab at Heaton shed on the day are John Arnott Brown (left) - an organiser of the special - and the driver. Picture John Arnott Brown courtesy The A1 Steam Locomotive Trust.

*Below*
No. 60145 has the road at Normanton station with the Healey Mills to Tyne Yard freight service in May 1965. At this time *Saint Mungo* was working from York and was based there from 1963 to the start of 1966 when leaving for Darlington, although the engine's final two months were spent at the aforementioned. Photograph by Roger Bastin courtesy The A1 Steam Locomotive Trust.

Y
168

60145

*Above*
Birmingham Moor Street station was an unlikely place to find an Eastern Region Pacific, yet at the end of steam anything could happen. The Warwickshire Railway Society managed to persuade the 'powers that be' to allow no. 60145 to start off the 'Hants and Dorset Rail Tour' on 5th September 1965, running as far as Banbury before returning later in the day after several other locomotives had been employed on the jaunt. Picture by Richard Postill.

*Opposite above*
Arriving at York with the up 'Flying Scotsman' on 29th December 1952 is no. 60145 *Saint Mungo*. The locomotive was allocated to Gateshead at this time and had been there from new in March 1949. Picture courtesy *Yorkshire Post Newspapers*.

*Opposite below*
To the east of Edinburgh at Prestonpans, *Saint Mungo* is at the head of the down Penzance to Aberdeen train on 20th June 1952. At approximately 785 miles, the service is the longest in Britain and still operates today, although uses one locomotive whereas several would have been employed in steam days; no. 60145 is perhaps working the Newcastle to Edinburgh portion.

THE
QUEEN OF SCOTS
60146
BRITISH RAILWAYS

60146
PEREGRINE
60146

*Above*
Despite the appearance of a dry day and the track being level at Doncaster station, no. 60146 *Peregrine* requires the assistance of the sanders to get the train, which was bound for London, moving on the 27th March 1952. After leaving Doncaster shed no. 60146 moved briefly to Copley Hill, then York in June 1950. Six months later the engine was named and took a recently discarded one from Gresley A4 Pacific no. 4903 (BR no. 60034) which took *Lord Faringdon*, after the Chairman of the GCR, later Deputy Chairman of the LNER. Picture courtesy *Yorkshire Post Newspapers*.

*Opposite above*
No. 60146 takes the up fast line through Doncaster station with the 'Queen of Scots Pullman' train during 1949. The engine had been turned out from Darlington in early April and for the first year in service worked from Doncaster shed. The 'Queen of Scots Pullman' had been reintroduced after the war and was usually made up from 10 carriages (400 tons), with arrival scheduled at King's Cross for 20.05.

*Opposite below*
From late April to the 10th May 1957 no. 60146 *Peregrine* had some minor issues fixed at Doncaster Works and while there Messrs Gold, Rowley and Sturrock were photographed with the engine. *Peregrine* returned to the shops a total of 23 times over 15 years in service, five of these being general repairs and five trips were made to the weigh house (four being in quick succession - three in 1955 and another in 1956).

60146

60146
PEREGRINE

*Above*
View north at the southern end of Newcastle Central station, which is in the shadow of not only no. 60147 *North Eastern*'s smoke but the large spire of St Mary's Cathedral. After the end of the Second World War the decision was taken to revert the 'Flying Scotsman' train to a stopping service all year round instead of becoming a non-stop express during the summer season as had been the case in LNER days. The up train had two stops between Edinburgh and King's Cross, one being Newcastle and the other Grantham, where engines and crews would be changed.

*Opposite above*
A long, mixed freight train trails behind no. 60146 through Normanton station during 1965. In 1963 the locomotive left York shed for three months during the summer, taking a holiday at Neville Hill shed before returning until condemned in October 1965. *Peregrine* still retains the nameplates, in spite of not being far from withdrawal, although the electric lights and generator have been discarded at some point; the smokebox number plate has also been moved and the top lamp bracket repositioned with split handrail. Photograph by Roger Bastin courtesy The A1 Steam Locomotive Trust.

*Opposite below*
No. 60146 *Peregrine* had the Christmas period off in 1959, spending a month in Doncaster Works for a general overhaul, which saw a fresh boiler fitted. This was diagram 118 no. 29868 that had previously been with Thompson A2/3 Class Pacific no. 60519 *Honeyway* and several Peppercorn A2 Class Pacifics. No. 60146 is seen on York station's west side on 5th January 1960. Photograph by D.J. Dippie.

*Below*
No. 60147 *North Eastern* was erected at Darlington in mid-April 1949 and had to wait longer than most to receive a name, which occurred in March 1952. Allocated to Gateshead when new, the engine remained there until late summer 1960. *North Eastern* is still carrying the shedplate in this picture taken in the late 1950s at Edinburgh Haymarket shed; Gresley A3 Pacific no. 60095 *Flamingo*, which was a long-term Carlisle Canal shed resident, is seen to the right of the engine. Photograph by Bill Reed.

*Above*
Heading north away from Sunderland at Portobello Lane, just north of Monkwearmouth station, is no. 60147 *North Eastern*. After leaving Gateshead the locomotive was allocated to Heaton, then in September 1962 transferred to Tweedmouth before moving south to York a year later. Following nearly a year at work there the engine was condemned and sent for scrapping at A. Draper's yard in Hull. Photograph by D.J. Dippie.

60148
ABOYEUR
60148

60148
THE

*Above*
No. 60158 *Aberdonian* has made way for no. 60148 *Aboyeur* to continue to King's Cross with the up 'Northumbrian' from Grantham station on 1st May 1953. The train's origin was Newcastle, leaving for King's Cross at 10.40 with arrival scheduled for 16.15, with stops at Darlington, York, Selby, Doncaster and Grantham. No. 60148 had spells at Copley Hill, Ardsley and Gateshead before being withdrawn from Ardsley in June 1965; the 'Northumbrian' did not survive much longer. Photograph by P.N. Townend.

*Opposite above*
No. 60148 *Aboyeur*'s vacuum pipe provides the impetus for the locomotive to be turned on King's Cross station's turntable during the early 1950s. The locomotive was sent into traffic from Darlington in May 1949 and was originally decorated in the LNER's apple green livery before switching to BR blue in January 1951 at the first general repair. A 35B shed code is on the smokebox door, denoting Grantham shed which had the locomotive on duty from September 1951 to August 1955, punctuated by a spell at Copley Hill between October 1953 and May 1954.

*Opposite below*
Another view of no. 60148 *Aboyeur* in King's Cross station's locomotive yard - the turntable is seen behind the locomotives on the left - as the engine takes on coal from the chute; an unidentified and immaculate A4 Pacific is next in line. *Aboyeur* is being prepared to take out the 'Aberdonian' which had an early evening departure time during the BR period and was scheduled to arrive in Aberdeen in the early morning.

*Below*
Although diagrammed for a V2 Class locomotive, the mid-afternoon King's Cross to Edinburgh goods train - popularly known as the 'Scotch Goods' - was often dispatched behind a Pacific locomotive of A1 and even A4 Classes. Leaving the goods yard at 15.15 the engine would run all the way to Newcastle where, after being relieved (and perhaps a few pints in the nearest pub), the crew would lodge and return to London the following day. On 30th May 1957 no. 60149 *Amadis* was rostered for the duty and is seen exiting the yard at King's Cross. Picture by P.N. Townend.

*Above*
*Amadis* leaves King's Cross through Belle Isle on 1st July 1958 with a special express to Middlesbrough for the launch of *Overseas Explorer* from the Furness Shipbuilding Co.'s yard on the Tees. The engine has been immaculately turned out by the staff at King's Cross for the occasion, but Gateshead's no. 60135 *Madge Wildfire*, which is seen behind exiting the shed yard, does nothing for that shed's reputation with regard to the general presentation of the engines allocated there. Picture by P.N. Townend.

No. 60149 entered traffic from Darlington in May 1949 and was named *Amadis* 18 months later after the winner of the 1909 Doncaster Cup. The engine spent many years subsequently racing up and down the east coast main line from several sheds, the last of which was Doncaster, accepting the locomotive on to the roster in late September 1958. *Amadis* is seen at King's Cross station on 1st September 1962, perhaps from the outer platform of the west side looking south west to the suburban station and St Pancras. In the centre is the Culross building, which was erected by the GNR and consisted of a number of flats for employees, and on the right is Pancras Gas Works. This area has recently been cleared for the redevelopment of St Pancras station. Picture by Eric Vogel courtesy The A1 Steam Locomotive Trust.

*Above*
Attention is received by no. 60149 outside Doncaster shed c. 1962. The locomotive's last general repair took place between 7th November and 22 December 1961 and (either impressively or through a lack of accurate record-keeping) another works visit for repair was not documented before withdrawal in June 1964. *Amadis* was subsequently scrapped by Cox & Danks in 1965.

*Below*
*Amadis* at the north end of Grantham station on 20th August 1958. Picture by Bill Reed.

60150
DN103
WILLBROOK

*Opposite above*
Heading south through Doncaster station is no. 60150 *Willbrook*, which is attached to an assorted group of carriages on 1st August 1953. The engine was only a short time away from being admitted to the town's works for a third general repair in as many years. Photograph by P.N. Townend.

*Opposite below*
Even though *Willbrook*'s smokebox door is open - an often telltale signal of an engine's withdrawal at the end of steam - on 13th August 1964 there was still two months of work to be performed before no. 60150's fate was sealed. *Willbrook* is seen at York shed, just west of the station, with the rail bridge for the Malton and Scarborough line over the River Ouse to the left of the buffer. Photograph by Bill Reed.

*Below*
No. 60150 *Wilbrook* has assembled a train of goods vans, as well as a couple of containers (behind the tender) at Sunderland Portobello Lane goods yard and is seen leaving there for York's Dringhouses Yard on 19th June 1962. The locomotive was employed at the city's shed at this time, arriving there in November 1960 and remaining until withdrawn in October 1964. Photograph by D.J. Dippie.

60150

60150

*Above*
Eighteen miles north of York no. 60151 *Midlothian* briefly breaks the tranquillity of Sessay station to rush through with the down Glasgow express on 13th February 1953. The section of track between York and Northallerton was quite straight and level allowing quite high speeds to be achieved and the locomotive looks to be moving at a fair rate here, with the exhaust from the double chimney being thrown above and away from the cab pleasingly. An oddity is the barrow adjacent to the down line for the station platform. Photograph courtesy *Yorkshire Post Newspapers.*

*Opposite above*
After being completed at Darlington in mid-June 1949 no. 60150 was allocated to Heaton shed, but less than a month later the locomotive was reallocated to Gateshead, remaining there for the next 11 years. *Willbrook* has worked from Newcastle to Edinburgh Waverley and is seen at the latter ready to leave for Glasgow in August 1952. Picture by Eric Treacy courtesy David Joy.

*Opposite below*
No. 60150 *Willbrook* simmers in the cold surroundings of Newcastle Central station on 13th February 1960. Nameplates were fitted to the locomotive in January 1951 and the name was taken from the winner of the Doncaster Cup of 1914. Whilst a good proportion of the Pacifics built by the LNER took their names from famous racehorses, the A4s and Peppercorn A1s were notable exceptions; only 13 of the latter were so honoured. Photograph by D.J. Dippie.

25

60151

*Above*
View from the down platform at Northallerton station on 19th April 1963 as no. 60151 *Midlothian* passes through with a King's Cross to Newcastle express. The Great North of England Railway opened the station on 31st March 1841 after costing over £1,500 to construct. Originally this only consisted of facilities on the up side of the line but as further lines were added in the decades following, a second platform on the down side, with a bay for the Hawes branch, supplemented the main building, which also saw additions to the structure. After the end of steam most of the down platform was removed. No. 60151 was erected a short distance away at Darlington at the end of June 1949 and was named in March 1951. Picture by Rev. J. David Benson courtesy The A1 Steam Locomotive Trust.

*Opposite above*
Just south of Gateshead, BR established Tyne marshalling yard as part of the Modernisation Plan. The facility opened in the early 1960s on the west side of the east coast main line, not far from Allerdene colliery; the headgear and huge spoil heap of the pit are visible in the background. No. 60151 *Midlothian* is seen heading north away from the yard during November 1964 with a freight train destined for Edinburgh. Only recently the engine had been transferred to Gateshead shed and would remain there until July 1965. Surprisingly, Tyne yard is still open and operated by DB Schenker, although the sidings now store coaching stock and track maintenance equipment in addition to freight traffic. The colliery site has since been completely remodelled and is the location of the famous 'Angel of the North' sculpture.

*Opposite below*
Standing next to an unidentified diesel locomotive at Edinburgh Haymarket shed on 3rd July 1961 is no. 60151 *Midlothian*. Over a year had been spent working from Heaton at this time and just over another year would elapse before the next move to Tweedmouth would occur. Following two years there *Midlothian* was sent to Gateshead and later ended 16 years in service at York, being condemned in November 1965. Photograph by Bill Reed.

*Below*

Although lacking identification at the front end, this victim of the Modernisation Plan is recognisable as no. 60152 *Holyrood* by the cab number. The date is 18th September 1965 and the locomotive had been missing from York shed's roster since mid-June; J. Cashmore had been contracted for disposal in August but had yet to perform the duty. No. 60155 *Borderer* is tender-to-tender with no. 60152 and was still in service at this time. However, by early October the engine had met a similar fate and would be disposed of by the end of the year. Both are seen to the west of York shed in sidings opposite Leeman Road and behind is the imposing water tower erected by the NER in 1909 which stood until 1973. Photograph by Bill Reed.

*Above*
Edinburgh Waverley was originally a relatively small station when opened by the North British Railway on 22nd June 1846. As traffic increased subsequently the NBR was obliged to considerably rebuild the station in the 1890s, costing well over £1 million. At this time the station was the largest in Britain and with 21 platforms could receive the large amounts of traffic arriving from England, which was received in the eastern half, and from Glasgow and northern Scotland - places such as Dundee and Aberdeen - in the opposite section. No. 60152 *Holyrood* is seen departing from the latter section at 16.04 on 27th July 1961 with a stopping train. The engine was allocated to Edinburgh Haymarket shed at this time and would remain there until September 1963. Picture by D.J. Dippie.

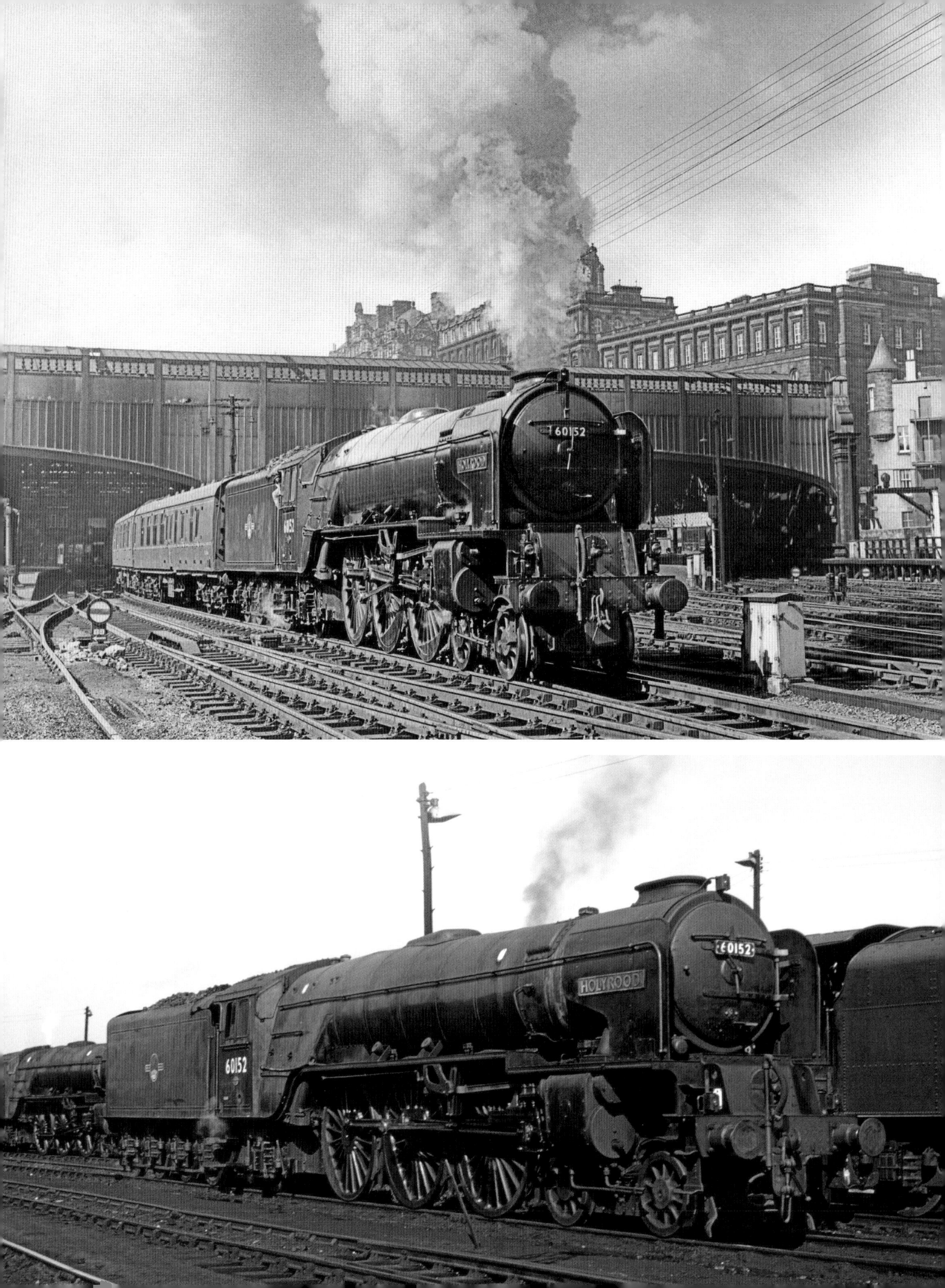
60152
HOLYROOD
60152
HOLYROOD
60152

*Above*
Another one of York shed's long-term residents was no. 60153 *Flamboyant*. Arriving from Doncaster Works in August 1949 the locomotive remained allocated to the depot until condemned in early November 1962. *Flamboyant* is seen here at York station having just taken over a service that had originated in East Anglia and was destined for Newcastle. Photograph by Eric Treacy courtesy David Joy.

*Opposite above*
Despite being in the no. 2 link at Haymarket shed, no. 60152 *Holyrood* has received some attention to bring the metalwork up to a nice shine for departure from Waverley station with the 12.00 train to Carlisle. *Holyrood* was allocated to Haymarket when new from Darlington in July 1949, but in early 1951 the engine was one of three A1s moved to Glasgow Polmadie shed, which was an ex-LMSR depot, and spent a short spell there before a further six-month allocation in December 1952. Picture by Eric Treacy courtesy David Joy.

*Opposite below*
Two months before being condemned for scrap no. 60152 has been captured in steam at York shed. *Holyrood* moved from Edinburgh St Margaret's shed in September 1964 after a year there to take up residence in England for the first time. In the main the engine had been maintained at Doncaster, but there was a trip to Darlington for weighing and two entries into Cowlairs Works, Glasgow, for minor repairs to be carried out, these taking place in 1951 and 1955. Photograph by Bill Reed.

A large contingent of 'spotters' have gathered at the end of a platform at King's Cross station to witness the departure of no. 60153 *Flamboyant* during September 1952. York A1s did not often work through to King's Cross in the early 1950s, but visits later became more frequent through changes in services of both freight and passenger varieties.

*Right*
Holmeside provides the vantage point to view no. 60153 leaving the south end of Sunderland station with an express on 15th March 1961. This area has since been built over and shops occupy the space. Photograph by D.J. Dippie.

*Below*
Whilst the photographer's view forward is obscured by exhaust, the driver of no. 60153 has no such problem as he takes his train out of York with an express for London. Photograph by Eric Treacy courtesy David Joy.

*Opposite above*
York-based no. 60154 *Bon Accord* is seen with a rake of empty carriages at Monkwearmouth, Sunderland on 2nd June 1962. The Pullman car behind the tender is *Phyllis*, which was a first class kitchen car built for the LNER in 1928 and remained in service until the mid-1960s. The carriage was then bought privately and currently awaits restoration. Picture by D.J. Dippie.

*Opposite below*
Built at Doncaster in late September 1949, no. 60154 returned to the workshops twice before the first general repair was undertaken between early March and mid-April 1951; this was also when the nameplates were fitted. The locomotive is seen in the Crimpsall yard at Doncaster during one of the two previous visits, which took place from late December 1949 to early January 1950 and late April 1950 - perhaps being the latter. Photograph by Malcolm Crawley.

*Below*
Heading north towards East Boldon and Newcastle, having passed through Seaburn, is no. 60154 *Bon Accord*. Seen on 15th July 1960, the locomotive was four months away from leaving Gateshead shed for York. Photograph by D.J. Dippie.

60 54
60154

*Left*
Fireman Tony Watson in the driver's seat of no. 60154 *Bon Accord*, which is about to leave Neville Hill shed to take on water in the yard. From July 1963 the locomotive was based at Neville Hill shed and was withdrawn from there in October 1965. Picture courtesy Tony Watson.

*Below*
Another view of *Bon Accord* moving empty carriages at Monkwearmouth on 2nd June 1962. There have been few alterations to the engine from new, apart from the addition of AWS apparatus, beading to the chimney and nameplates. Picture by D.J. Dippie.

Two views of no. 60155 *Borderer* heading south from just north of Doncaster station with a train of mineral wagons on 10th April 1965. Travelling on the main line, no. 60155 is seen passing under the Doncaster avoiding line in the top image and below is about to cross the bridge over the River Don, whilst in the distance is North Bridge Road (a new road bridge has since been built and crosses the main line between the two aforementioned bridges). *Borderer* was six months away from being condemned at York shed. Photograph by Roger Bastin courtesy The A1 Steam Locomotive Trust.

Despite appearing to be in steam no. 60155 *Borderer* has not been moved for a time as there is a build up of oxidisation on the leading bogie wheel and rear coupled wheel. Seen at York on 3rd April 1965 no. 60155 is missing the right-hand side works plate which would reveal that the engine was erected at Doncaster in September 1949 and was works no. 2049. Photograph by Bill Reed.

*Above*
Again seen at York shed, *Borderer* appears to be out of service once more but on this occasion - 18th September 1965 - a return to traffic would seem highly unlikely, being shorn of all relevant identification at the front end. No. 60155 was officially withdrawn on 4th October. Picture by Bill Reed.

*Below*
View from the rear of the houses on Newbury Street, Monkwearmouth, to the footbridge linking Bartram Street and Hilda Street/Longfield Road. No. 60155 *Borderer* heads south towards Sunderland station with an express on 20th June 1960; the locomotive was Gateshead-allocated at this time. Picture by D.J. Dippie.

60156

60156
GREAT CENTRAL
60156

*Above*
On King's Cross station's turntable being manoeuvred into position for the next service c. 1955 is no. 60156.

*Opposite above*
Grantham resident no. 60156 *Great Central* departs from Doncaster station with a stopping service to Grantham. Judging by the engine's condition and the train being worked, a general repair has occurred and no. 60156 is being gently run-in before being passed for regular service. Photograph by Eric Treacy courtesy David Joy.

*Opposite below*
No. 60156 was one of a group of Peppercorn A1s named after four of the constituent companies of the LNER. The omissions were the Great North of Scotland Railway and Great Northern Railway, although the latter was already in use by Thompson A1/1 no. 60113. All concerned had the company's crest displayed above the name. *Great Central* is seen at Grantham station c. 1960.

60156
GREAT CENTRAL
60156

*Above*
Originally allocated to King's Cross shed, no. 60156 remained there for nearly two years before being transferred north to Grantham where another five years were spent at work on the mainline expresses - the engine was working from there when pictured here leaving King's Cross station with the 'Flying Scotsman'. A return was then made to King's Cross where three more years of sterling work was performed in the shadow of the shed's more illustrious residents, the Gresley A4s. P.N. Townend - in his excellent book *Top Shed* - recounts that *Great Central* amassed 96,000 miles in one year and the 12 A1s based at King's Cross in the late 1950s averaged 1,600 miles per month more than the A4s. Despite such assured performances, no. 60156 was moved to Doncaster in April 1959 and then York in January 1964 before being condemned for scrap in May 1965.

*Opposite*
No. 60156 *Great Central* stands resplendent in fresh livery outside Doncaster shed. Erected at the town's works in late October 1949, the engine would return a further 18 times for repairs and maintenance over 16 years in traffic. A total of seven general repairs were carried out and the same number of replacement boilers were fitted, with five coming from other A1s, one from an A2 and another from A2/2 no. 60506 *Wolf of Badenoch*, but this was a diagram 118 type and not diagram 106A usually fitted to that class. *Great Central* had been sent into service with BR blue livery and this lasted until July 1952 when BR green was first applied; the name was also fitted at this time.

*Above*
A swarm of young locomotive enthusiasts has gathered around no. 60157 *Great Eastern*, whilst one too young to loiter at the end of one of King's Cross station's many platforms has been escorted by his parents. The driver looks none too impressed by the attention and there was perhaps always a lottery as to whether the crew would be approachable for a cab inspection. Nevertheless, getting a close-up view of the cab and a blast of heat from the fire was undoubtedly a highlight of the day for these youngsters - and some a bit older as well. The date is during 1954 when no. 60157 was allocated to Grantham. Picture by Geoff Parrish courtesy The A1 Steam Locomotive Trust.

*Opposite below*
Sharing a similar allocation history to *Great Central*, *Great Eastern* attained one of the highest mileages between general repairs by any engine allocated to King's Cross according to P.N. Townend in *Top Shed* - 197,000. Generally, the A1s were expected to complete 18 months in traffic before entering works for repair and, in the main, no. 60157 stuck to this pattern apart from once when the locomotive went from April 1956 to October 1958 before undergoing a heavy overhaul. However, this should be qualified by noting that minor repairs were carried out at Doncaster and even complicated issues could be dealt with by King's Cross shed without the locomotive travelling to the works.

*Above*

No. 60157 *Great Eastern* runs down the platform at Grantham station with an up express on 9th April 1964. As with classmate no. 60156 *Great Central*, no. 60157 was transferred to Doncaster from King's Cross in early April 1959 but remained there until withdrawn in January 1965. Picture by Cedric Clayson courtesy The A1 Steam Locomotive Trust.

60157

157

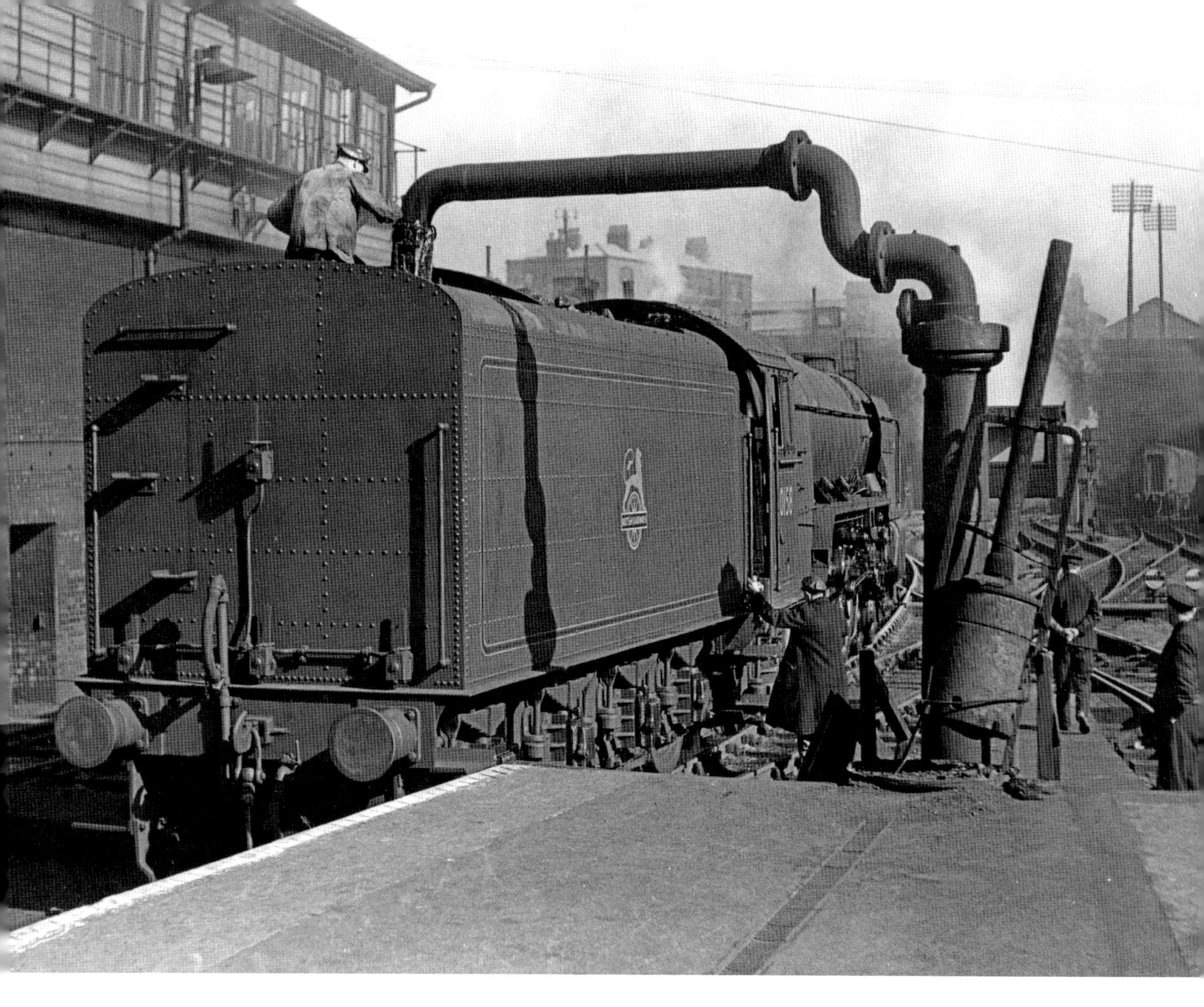

*Above*
No. 60158 *Aberdonian* takes on water before being attached to the northbound 'White Rose' express on the east side of King's Cross station, c. 1953. Picture by Eric Treacy courtesy David Joy.

*Opposite*
For many years locomotives were generally scrapped at a railway company's own workshops, given the relatively small volume dealt with, the ability to recycle parts, etc. When the timeframe for the enactment of BR's Modernisation Plan was brought forward in the late 1950s there were suddenly large numbers of locomotives accumulating for processing by the workshops' scrapyards. To clear the backlog and reduce the workload, the decision was taken to invite bids for redundant engines from private scrap merchants and by the early 1960s dozens of firms, both large and small, were involved in dismantling the steam fleet. A. Draper Ltd, Hull, was relatively late to the process in 1964, but soon made up for lost time by scrapping large volumes of classes from all regions, only finishing at the start of the 1970s. Unsurprisingly, the A1s found their way there and no. 60157 was one, being pictured at the Sculcoates site (interestingly formerly a goods station) on 7th March 1965 as the engine's heart is ripped out bit by bit; work has yet to begin on the recovery of the copper firebox - the most valuable item. Of note is the working conditions for the men, especially the asbestos boiler lagging which has been unwittingly left in place. Both pictures by Revd J. David Benson courtesy The A1 Steam Locomotive Trust.

THE FLYING SCOTSMAN
60158
ABERDONIAN

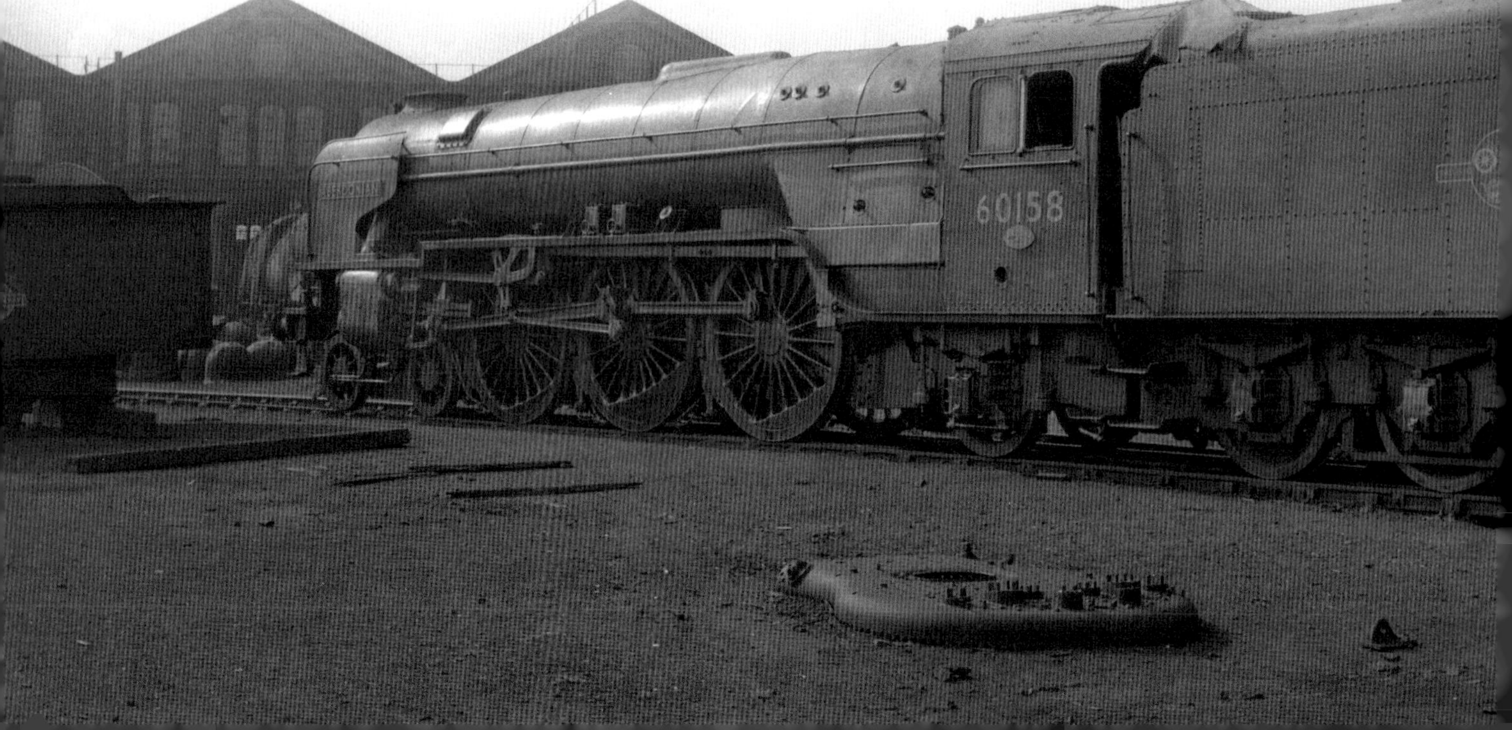
60158

*Above*
The driver of no. 60158 *Aberdonian* has spotted the camera, which is positioned to the south of Holgate Road bridge (built in Derby by Handyside in 1911) looking north to York station, and happily smiles as he passes by around 1952. The Grantham-allocated engine is at the head of the up 'Northumbrian'; this usually consisted of 13 carriages with restaurant facilities for first and third class. *Aberdonian* was based at Grantham twice in 15 years' service, the first period was from September 1951 to June 1953, then returning in May 1954 until June 1957. Photograph by Eric Treacy courtesy David Joy.

*Opposite above*
With the long formation of the 'Flying Scotsman' at Newcastle Central station on 14th April 1958 is no. 60158 *Aberdonian*. Picture by D.J. Dippie.

*Opposite below*
No. 60158 *Aberdonian* makes an unscheduled visit to Doncaster Works on 14th July 1957. The engine had been admitted for similar attention earlier in the year and would return in early October for a general overhaul to be carried out.
No. 60158 was allocated to King's Cross shed at this time (June 1957 to September 1958). Photograph by Bill Reed.

*Opposite*
View from the platform at Edinburgh Haymarket station as no. 60159 *Bonnie Dundee* arrives with a stopping train on 13th September 1955. The station was originally the terminus of the Edinburgh & Glasgow Railway when opened in the early 1840s, but this importance was short lived as the route had been extended to Waverley by the middle of the decade. On the left is Haymarket Ice Rink, which was open from 1912 to 1978. Photograph by Bill Reed.

*Opposite below*
Allocated to Edinburgh Haymarket shed from new in November 1949 until September 1963, *Bonnie Dundee* is seen at the depot on 26th August 1958. Picture by D.J. Dippie.

*Below*
No. 60159 *Bonnie Dundee* heads west through Princes Street Gardens with the 17.10 express to Aberdeen on 13th September 1957. The A1s were the last of a number of classes used to work the heavy northern expresses over the difficult terrain between Edinburgh and the 'Granite City'. Photograph by B.W.L. Brooksbank.

60159

60159
BONNIE DUNDEE
60159

60160
AULD REEKIE
60160

60160
AULD REEKIE
60160

*Above*
Leading a train bound for Glasgow from Waverley station is no. 60160 *Auld Reekie*. Constructed at Doncaster in early December 1949, the locomotive was based at Haymarket until September 1963, but had two spells at Polmadie depot in 1951. Withdrawal from Edinburgh St Margaret's occurred in December 1963.

*Opposite above*
No. 60160 *Auld Reekie* stands at the southern end of Aberdeen Ferryhill shed's coal stage in order to receive fuel for the return journey to the capital city on 16th June 1962. The ramped coal stage was installed in the early 1900s when the new shed was built on the west side of the line to the city; the fuelling point was on the eastern side of the shed. Picture by Bill Reed.

*Opposite below*
No. 60160 took the name *Auld Reekie* in March 1951, this being the epithet given to the Scottish capital in the 18th century and subsequently carried forward into everyday vocabulary. Despite the unflattering name, no. 60160 is neatly presented for the day's work, which is to be undertaken following the change of signal that will allow the engine to head off from Haymarket shed and run up to Waverley station. Interestingly, the locomotive had few visits to Doncaster Works - eight over 14 years for general repairs - and only two trips were made to Cowlairs Works for additional attention, both taking place in 1951. Picture by Bill Reed.

THE
QUEEN OF SCOTS
60161
NORTH BRITISH
60161

60161
NORTH BRITISH

*Above*
Sweeping down Cockburnspath bank with the down 'Heart of Midlothian' at the end of the 1950s is no. 60161 *North British*. The fireman was perhaps quite thankful that the service was not heading in the opposite direction as the formidable incline had a rising gradient of 1 in 96. The remainder of the route to Edinburgh was quite straightforward, in spite of several undulations of the terrain, but the final few hundred yards to Waverley required a 1 in 78 to be negotiated.

*Opposite above*
No. 60161 *North British* is depicted in the servicing area at the eastern end of Edinburgh Waverley station, before taking over the up 'Queen of Scots' train as far as Newcastle during the early 1950s. The service usually consisted of eight carriages which left Glasgow Queen Street station at 10.50 to reach Edinburgh for a departure at 12.00. Two hours and eighteen minutes were scheduled for the 124 miles to Newcastle and the same time was allowed from there to Leeds. The final leg to King's Cross was non-stop and arrival was to be at 20.05. Picture by Eric Treacy courtesy David Joy.

*Opposite below*
Not yet a St Margaret's engine, no. 60161 *North British* was still allocated to Haymarket when captured at the ash pits at Aberdeen Ferryhill shed on 10th May 1963. The Caledonian Railway erected the depot, which replaced an earlier establishment, in the late 1890s and a fragile agreement existed between the company and the North British Railway for the latter's engines to be accommodated and serviced there. This was subsequently continued by the LMSR and LNER up to the formation of BR. No. 60161 would make a final journey to Aberdeen after withdrawal in October 1963 to Inverurie Works (north west of the city) for scrapping, following no. 60159 *Bonnie Dundee* which was cut up there a few months earlier. Photograph by Bill Reed.

*Opposite*
The hard work is nearly over for no. 60162 *Saint Johnstoun* as the engine reaches Whitrope summit following an 11-mile climb of difficult gradients from Hawick on the Waverley route. No. 60162 is seen at the southern end of Whitrope tunnel with the early afternoon train to Carlisle during the opening years of the 1960s.

*Below*
Departing from Newcastle Central station with a northbound King's Cross to Glasgow express is no. 60162 *Saint Johnstoun*. The name, which was fitted to the locomotive in August 1951, had previously been carried by NBR Reid Atlantic (LNER C11) no. 901 as *St. Johnstoun* (withdrawn December 1937) - both were nevertheless the alternative name of Perth. Picture by Eric Treacy courtesy David Joy.

*Page 160 above*
The comings and goings at Edinburgh Waverley continue uninterrupted despite track work taking place on one of the western lines and no. 60162 *Saint Johnstoun* gets away with a train to Aberdeen. Seen in the early 1950s, the engine has lost the electric lights and generator but is still well turned out with highly burnished smokebox door hinges and buffers, which are undoubtedly the sign of a crew taking great pride in their locomotive. Photograph by Eric Treacy courtesy David Joy.

*Page 160 below*
No. 60162 *Saint Johnstoun* departs from Glasgow Queen Street station with the 'Queen of Scots' Pullman on 11th October 1958. The engine is about to tackle the 1 in 42-gradient tunnel which was built because the Forth & Clyde Canal owners would not allow the Edinburgh & Glasgow Railway to bridge the waterway to the north. This resulted in trains having to be assisted by ropes out of the station for around 60 years after opening. In later years assistance to the top of the incline was often provided by one of Eastfield shed's N15 Class 0-6-2Ts. Picture by P.N. Townend.

60162

60162

*Above*
Peppercorn A2 Class Pacific no. 525 reverses out of Doncaster Works on 9th December 1947 to head down to Doncaster Carr shed for coaling and then begin running-in before entering service just before Christmas. The engine was decorated in LNER apple green livery when new and did not receive BR blue subsequently, but had BR green from August 1949 after the first general repair took place.

*Below*
At the start of the summer season 1948 no. 525 - now carrying the name *A.H. Peppercorn* - is seen at King's Cross station with an early evening train ready to head north to Leeds. For the first 12 months the locomotive was employed at Doncaster shed, then being transferred to Peterborough New England depot.

Renumbered 60525 in August 1949, *A.H. Peppercorn* was removed from Peterborough New England during the same month to enjoy the picturesque scenery of north-east Scotland at the end of summer. The transfer was part of a general reallocation of some Thompson A2/2s which were struggling on the Edinburgh to Aberdeen line. No. 60525 remained allocated to Aberdeen - the engine is seen here at the city's station - until withdrawn in March 1963.

*Above*
No. 526 *Sugar Palm* was the second Peppercorn Pacific to be erected at Doncaster, also being the first built there under BR, entering traffic in early January 1948. At this time the engine was very much the same as no. 525, but at the first general repair (from 13th September to 27th October 1949) *Sugar Palm* received a Kylchap blastpipe and double chimney as well as a multiple valve regulator. No. 60526 (from August 1948) is seen leaving York with an express for Newcastle in the late 1950s. Photograph by Eric Treacy courtesy David Joy.

No. 60526 *Sugar Palm* only spent nine days allocated to York shed before being sent to Leeds Neville Hill depot where eight months were spent at work. *Sugar Palm* was then returned to York, remaining there until condemned in November 1962 and the locomotive was subsequently scrapped at Doncaster. No. 60526 is seen at York station around 1960. Photograph by Bill Reed.

*Above*
By the time no. E527 *Sun Chariot* had been completed at Doncaster towards the end of January 1948, BR had introduced the regional prefixes for numbering and the engine was the first of five A2s to receive this. Only six months later *Sun Chariot* took BR number 60527 and is seen with this just over a year later racing across the Forth Bridge with an express for Edinburgh Waverley.

*Below*
For the benefit of the photographer a diesel shunter at Aberdeen Ferryhill shed has kindly pulled out Gresley V2 no. 60898 and - the focus of this shot - no. 60527 *Sun Chariot* on 16th June 1962. The locomotive arrived at the depot at the end of May 1960 and spent over three years there. Picture by Bill Reed.

SUN CHARIOT
60527

*Above*
Climbing up to Whitrope summit at Shankend - and approaching the viaduct - is no. 60527 *Sun Chariot*, which has charge of an express from Edinburgh bound for Carlisle. Allocated to Dundee at this time, the locomotive was a good distance from home and has perhaps been borrowed for the service. Picture by Eric Treacy courtesy David Joy.

*Opposite*
No. 60527 has a few weeks to go before the locomotive's final repair was completed at Darlington on 21st August 1964, being pictured here in the Repair Shop on 9th August; A4 no. 60024 *Kingfisher* is in the berth on the left. The engine had already spent nearly two months at Darlington which seems quite unusual even when taking into account the phasing out of steam repairs at the time. Being largely allocated to Scottish sheds, *Sun Chariot* made several visits to Cowlairs in addition to Doncaster and also made a rare visit to Gateshead Works. Photograph by N.W. Skinner courtesy J.W. Armstrong Trust.

*Below and opposite above*
Two views of no. 60528 *Tudor Minstrel* at Perth station on 20th August 1965. The picture opposite shows the locomotive at the head of an up express under the main section of the station which was on the line between Glasgow and Aberdeen via Forfar - on the right are the platforms for trains running on the Perth to Dundee line, with a DMU having just arrived from the latter. The image below sees *Tudor Minstrel* taking the express under St Leonard's Bridge. At this time no. 60528 was based at Dundee shed and resided there from June 1961 to April 1966. The locomotive then spent two months at Aberdeen before withdrawal in early June 1966. Both Photographs by Bill Reed.

*Opposite below*
No. 60528 *Tudor Minstrel* at Perth with the 13.30 Aberdeen to Glasgow express on 3rd May 1966. Photograph by M. Dunnett courtesy of J.W. Armstrong Trust.

60528

60528

60528
BRITISH RAILWAYS

TUDOR MINSTREL
60528

*Above*
No. 60529 *Pearl Diver* sets off from Edinburgh Waverley station with the up 'Queen of Scots' Pullman during August 1954. Fitted with a Kylchap double chimney and multiple valve regulator in September 1949, the shafts to operate the latter is seen here running along the top side of the boiler from the cab to the header behind the chimney. Picture by Eric Treacy courtesy David Joy.

*Opposite above*
No. 60528 began service in late February 1948 as no. E528, being renumbered in June. The numbering used on the cab side was a larger variant than had previously been applied and is noticeably different from the 'British Railways' lettering on the tender, which had been placed on the sides when *Tudor Minstrel* was new; only the first two A2s had 'LNER' lettering. No. 60528 is seen at Chaloner's Whin Junction (where the Leeds line and the main line diverge south of York) with a lunchtime express from King's Cross to Newcastle on 10th July 1948.

*Opposite below*
In late summer 1958 no. 60528 is one of several engines assembled at Doncaster shed waiting to be taken into works; the locomotive behind is A1 no. 60148 *Aboyeur*. This was the sixth general repair for *Tudor Minstrel* and a further two would be undertaken before the locomotive was condemned. No. 60528 went four years between the final one and scrapping, although light attention was received at Darlington in the first half of 1965 and just over three months were recorded in the shops. Picture by Bill Reed.

Another view of no. 60529 on Haymarket shed's turntable. Allocated to the depot from new in February 1948, the locomotive did not find new accommodation until October 1961 at St Margaret's shed, which was a relatively short distance to the east of Waverley station. Photograph by Bill Reed.

*Above*
After arriving at Edinburgh Haymarket shed, c. 1960, the tender of no. 60529 *Pearl Diver* would be replenished from the mechanical coaler, which was located alongside the main line between Edinburgh and Glasgow. In the next step the engine was turned and took a free space outside the shed to receive water. Then, attention was given to the fire and the oil points checked (as well as the general condition of the locomotive) before travelling back to Waverley for the next train. Picture by Bill Reed.

*Below*
No. 60529 *Pearl Diver* was condemned in late December 1962, but subsequently languished for 18 months until purchased by G.H. Campbell, Airdrie, to reclaim the metal. Seen on 6th August 1963, *Pearl Diver* still had some time left to serve in purgatory (in this instance Bathgate shed, between Edinburgh and Glasgow) before the final act was carried out. Photograph by D.J. Dippie.

60530

*Above*
No. 60530 *Sayajirao* under attention in Darlington Works Repair Shop on 26th September 1964. The locomotive had arrived at the start of the month and was finished by the end of the first week of October. Occasional visits were made to Cowlairs, but these were significantly outweighed by 14 trips to Doncaster Works for maintenance. No. 60530 made an out of course visit to the latter in early 1954 after a serious derailment had occurred on 17th December 1953 whilst working an up freight service at Longniddry, south of Prestonpans, around 15 miles from Edinburgh. *Sayajirao* struck a length of metal that had fallen from an earlier freight train and left the line at speed, subsequently crashing into the station platform and then falling down an embankment. Sadly, the fireman was killed and the driver received life-changing injuries. The locomotive was repaired by the end of February 1954. Picture by N.W. Skinner courtesy J.W. Armstrong Trust.

*Opposite above*
No. 60530 *Sayajirao* heads west with an express past Edinburgh Haymarket shed, c. 1962. The locomotive was erected at Doncaster in early March 1948, as works no. 2021, and up to the end of the year was allocated to King's Cross shed. After a further year at Peterborough, no. 60530 relocated to Scotland and remained employed in the country until withdrawn. Photograph by Bill Reed.

*Opposite below*
Moving towards Aberdeen Ferryhill shed's turntable, which was located on the south west side of the site at the end of the road adjacent to the coal stage, is no. 60530 *Sayajirao*. Picture by Bill Reed.

60530
SAYAJIRAO
61293
60530
DUNDEE

60530

*Above*
The passengers of the up 'Aberdonian' have some delightful scenery to admire as no. 60531 *Bahram* works hard to get the train moving away from Aberdeen on the steeply graded section south through Cove Bay during August 1951. Much of the route between Edinburgh and Aberdeen was against the locomotive and before the 1930s much of the traffic was double headed. To eliminate this practice Gresley introduced the P2 Class 2-8-2s and these were aided by the V2s subsequently. After the former were rebuilt the A2s took over much of the work on the line and excelled until the demise of steam.

*Opposite above*
Steam is still in abundance at Dundee shed on 3rd June 1966. Standing next to Thompson B1 no. 61293 is no. 60530 *Sayajirao* which was transferred to the depot in July 1964 and remained there until November 1966, being the penultimate A2 Pacific left in traffic at the time. The B1 was also allocated to Dundee and had been there from new in February 1948; withdrawal occurred slightly earlier than no. 60530 in August 1966 - both were sold to Motherwell Machinery & Scrap Co. Photograph by Bill Reed.

*Opposite below*
View north from Dundee shed yard, with no. 60530 *Sayajirao* featured, on 2nd April 1966. For 11 years after leaving Peterborough the locomotive worked from Haymarket shed, then spending nearly two years at Edinburgh St Margarets. For just under a year Glasgow Polmadie shed retained the engine before final allocation to Dundee. The depot was located a short distance to the west of Dundee station (formerly Dundee Tay Bridge) on the shoreline between the running lines for the aforementioned and Dundee West station and the goods yards. Photograph by B.W.L. Brooksbank.

*Above*
At 11.00 on 4th August 1961 no. 60531 was captured between duties at Glasgow St Rollox shed. After being completed in March 1948 the engine spent time at Gateshead before heading to Aberdeen in August 1949. *Bahram* was condemned in mid-December 1962. Picture by D.J. Dippie.

*Below*
*Bahram* at Doncaster Works - fresh from a general repair - on 11th November 1955. Picture by Bill Reed.

Two views of no. 60532 *Blue Peter* going on and moving off Haymarket shed's turntable, around 1960. Carrying a 61B shed plate for Aberdeen Ferryhill, the locomotive was based there from January 1951 until June 1961 when transferred south to Dundee. A return was briefly made to Aberdeen in December 1966, but withdrawal had occurred by the end of the month. Both pictures by Bill Reed.

60532
S.W.L
40
Tons.
A-2.
YORK

*Above*
No. 60532 was stored for a time after being condemned by BR before being bought by Geoff Drury and Brian Hollingsworth. Funds were required for the locomotive's restoration and after a public appeal, aided by the BBC Television programme of the same name, *Blue Peter* entered Doncaster Works in May 1969. No. 60532 underwent a light overhaul and was repainted before a renaming ceremony (depicted here) which was scheduled for 22 November 1970.

*Opposite above*
Travelling south at Aberdeen (past the engine shed, with Ferryhill Junction signal box in the background) at the head of the up 'Aberdonian' is no. 60532 *Blue Peter* during late summer 1951. Completed at Doncaster in late March 1948 the engine was initially allocated to York where 18 months were spent on the roster before Edinburgh Haymarket took on the engine. Just before this move *Blue Peter* was taken into Doncaster Works for the first general repair to take place and subsequently returned to traffic with a double chimney and multiple valve regulator.

*Opposite below*
No. 60532 is wheeled in the Crimpsall Repair Shop in 1970. Following the restoration, the locomotive was mainly a display item and was subsequently stored out of service until 1986. At this time the North Eastern Locomotive Preservation Group took on the difficult task of repairing and restoring *Blue Peter*. Commendably, this was a success in only five years and the locomotive spent eight of the following ten years hauling railtours across the country; two years were lost following a disastrous wheelslip that ruined much of the motion and badly damaged the driving wheels. For the last 15 years no. 60532 has again been out of service, but in 2014 the engine was purchased by the Royal Scot Locomotive & General Trust which hopes to have *Blue Peter* in service again in the near future.

*Opposite above*
No. 60533 *Happy Knight* heads an express at Bawtry, south of Doncaster c. 1960. Picture by Bill Reed.

*Opposite below*
The up 'White Rose' express from Leeds to King's Cross pauses at the only stop on the journey south - Doncaster - on 4th June 1956, with no. 60533 *Happy Knight* leading the train. Recently allocated to Grantham, *Happy Knight* had been at Peterborough New England and Copley Hill, Leeds, on several occasions previously and would also reside at King's Cross and Doncaster before being removed from traffic in June 1963 - undoubtedly with the most transfers of any A2 Pacific. Photograph by Eric Treacy courtesy David Joy.

*Below*
Built at Doncaster in April 1948, no. 60533 was equipped with a double chimney and multiple valve regulator some 18 months later. The latter apparatus had a total of five valves fixed to the superheater header, which resulted in the projection seen behind the chimney, and was intended to give finer control of steam allowed to the cylinders as well as keeping steam circulating in the elements, stopping them from burning. The experience with the equipment allowed BR to fit the apparatus to the 'Britannia' Class Pacifics. Photograph by Bill Reed.

60533

60533
60533

*Above*
In the company of A3 Pacifics no. 60067 *Ladas* (left) and no. 60109 *Hermit* (right) at King's Cross shed on 15th October 1962 is no. 60533 *Happy Knight*. Photograph by Bill Reed.

*Opposite above*
No. 60534 *Irish Elegance* gets away from the east side of Edinburgh Waverley with an up express. Continuing the Doncaster tradition of naming Pacifics after racehorses, no. 60534 took *Irish Elegance* from the highly rated winner of the Royal Hunt Cup at Ascot and Portland Handicap (Doncaster) both in 1919.

*Opposite below*
A Thompson B1 waits to use the turntable at Edinburgh Haymarket shed as no. 60534 takes precedence on 11th April 1957. Picture by Bill Reed.

60534
60534
VIROL

60534

No. 60534 *Irish Elegance* is seen at Perth Shed during 1961. In mid-November of this year, the locomotive was transferred to a new shed for the first time since November 1949 when leaving York for Edinburgh Haymarket and in this instance moved across the Scottish capital to St Margaret's depot. No. 60534 left traffic while there in late December 1962. Picture courtesy Colour Rail.

*Above*
No. 60535 *Hornets Beauty* has fallen foul of the 'Big Freeze' of 1962/1963 and has been abandoned near Whitrope summit on the Waverley route. The engine would later return to service in the employ of St Margaret's shed.

*Below*
Entering traffic from Doncaster in May 1948, *Hornets Beauty* was sent to York shed where the engine is perhaps pictured a short time later. Decorated in LNER apple green, the change to BR green occurred in May 1950. Photograph by Eric Treacy courtesy David Joy.

*Above*
No. 60535 experienced a slight wheel slip when coming off an up express at Newcastle Central station on 4th November 1960. The engine had been in Doncaster Works around six weeks earlier and would be in service another 18 months before the final repair took place. Picture by D.J. Dippie.

*Opposite above*
The track gang at work on the west side of Edinburgh Waverley station down tools for a few moments to allow no. 60536 *Trimbush* to leave with an early afternoon express for Aberdeen, around 1953. Photograph by Eric Treacy courtesy David Joy.

*Below*
Seen in an immaculate condition outside the fitting shed at Haymarket is no. 60535 *Hornets Beauty*. This shed was built on to the north end of the depot just after World War Two, adding a further two roads, which could be accessed from both ends. Photograph by Bill Reed.

The fitters at Edinburgh Haymarket shed have been at work on no. 60536 *Trimbush*, removing the left-hand side piston and motion on 2nd July 1961. Only being released from Doncaster Works two months earlier, the locomotive has accumulated an admirable amount of dirt in that period. Photograph by Bill Reed.

*Above*
Alongside a Gresley V2 at Edinburgh Waverley station about 1961/1962 is no. 60536. From leaving Doncaster Works in mid-May 1948 to being condemned at the shops in December 1962, *Trimbush* had been repaired a total of 18 times and had six general repairs. Only four boilers were carried from new and this was quite a low figure in relation to the rest of the class - no. 60529 *Pearl Diver* had the least at two, followed by no. 60532 *Blue Peter* with three - which generally had seven boilers during their lifetimes (no. 60530 *Sayajirao* had the most at eight). No. 60536 is seen carrying a diagram 117 boiler with steam dome which was previously used by no. 60524 *Herringbone*. Picture courtesy Colour Rail.

*Opposite above*
No. 60537 *Bachelors Button* is seen on the turntable at King's Cross station not too long from entering service in June 1948; note the unorthodox (for the Eastern Region) disc headcode in use. The engine has the large type cab numbering with smaller 'British Railways' lettering.

*Opposite below*
Haymarket's *Bachelors Button* starts away from Newcastle Central station with a down express on 11th June 1960, but the locomotive seems to be experiencing a wheelslip. Picture by D.J. Dippie.

60537
60537
BRITISH RAILWAYS

60537

*Above*
No. 60537 *Bachelors Button* is moving on to the connecting track from Haymarket shed's turntable and coaler to the lines in the shed yard; the track on the extreme left was for Glasgow to Edinburgh traffic. The original shed was opened by the Edinburgh & Glasgow Railway in the late 1840s and was subsequently replaced nearly 50 years later by the North British Railway. This building had eight tracks, which could be accessed from both east and west ends, and was 91 metres long by 36 metres wide; a 50 ft turntable and ramped coal stage were also installed. By the 1930s further improvements were undertaken including the provision of a 500-ton mechanical coaler - costing £15,000 from Henry Lees & Co. - water tank and 70 ft turntable. Stanier Class 5 4-6-0 no. 45361 can be seen using the latter apparatus behind no. 60537 in this image, taken around 1951.

*Opposite*
No. 60537 *Bachelors Button* on Edinburgh Haymarket shed's turntable. Photograph by Bill Reed.

VELOCITY
D9003
60538

*Above*
Ex-works from Doncaster in early June 1956, *Velocity* is seen later in the month at Drem station, east of Edinburgh, near the junction with the line to North Berwick. No. 60538 had been fitted with Kylchap blastpipes and chimney, in addition to the multiple valve regulator, at the first general repair which was completed in October 1949 and was also given a coat of BR green at this time. The carriages behind the tender are in a fine state and the 'blood and custard' livery shines despite the weather looking decidedly overcast. Picture courtesy Colour Rail.

*Opposite above*
The last generation of steam express locomotive meets a first generation diesel express locomotive at Edinburgh Haymarket in June 1962. The Eastern Region took to the powerful English Electric 'Deltic' design after this had been dismissed by the London Midland Region, which turned to electrification. The authorities saw the 'Deltic' as ideal for the new high speed services envisaged due to the high horsepower rating of the locomotives. A total of 22 were ordered, entering service between February 1961 and May 1962; D9003 *Meld* was completed in late March 1961 and was in service until the end of 1980. No. 60538 *Velocity* had just less than six months left in traffic before being condemned at only 14 years old. Picture courtesy Colour Rail.

*Opposite below*
Another view of no. 60538 *Velocity* at Edinburgh Haymarket shed during June 1962, taken from the depot's turntable, which would become redundant following the shed's closure to steam in late 1963. At this time the facilities were modified to accommodate the growing Deltic and other diesel classes; a Type Four, later Class 40, can be seen with the front end just protruding from the interior of the shed. No. 60538 was not based at Haymarket and was only visiting from Tweedmouth, where a berth had been occupied from October 1961. Picture courtesy Colour Rail.

*Above*
No. 60538 *Velocity* heads north away from Durham station with an express on 16th July 1960. Only two months earlier the locomotive had been transferred from Gateshead, which received *Velocity* when new in mid-June 1948, to Heaton and from there the move to Tweedmouth occurred. Picture by D.J. Dippie.

*Opposite above*
Despite being one of the most important places on the Great Northern Railway, Doncaster was not provided with an adequate engine shed until 1876, when a 12-road through building was erected using bricks to the south of the station, which had been the location of the meagre facilities previously. By the time no. 60539 *Bronzino* was captured at the depot during September 1958 the roof has succumbed to old age and BR was in the process of modernising the facilities, partially with a view to the incoming diesel locomotives. Nevertheless, steam continued to be served there until mid-1966; *Bronzino* had been scrapped at Doncaster Works three and a half years earlier. Photograph by Bill Reed.

*Opposite below*
Gateshead Works was once the centre of locomotive matters for the North Eastern Railway, but a lack of space at the site resulted in Darlington taking much of the responsibility during the early 20th century. Gateshead then took on a secondary role as a maintenance facility and was a casualty of the economic depression of the late 1920s/early 1930s. The Second World War saw the shops revived and these subsequently continued to perform minor repairs for locomotives up to the late 1950s. No. 60539 is seen with motion in pieces on 10th October 1954 as an unofficial visit takes place, although at least two other A2s made official visits when allocated to sheds in the area. Picture by F.W. Hampson courtesy J.W. Armstrong Trust.

60539
60539

60539

*Above*
Two and a half miles south of Retford, no. 60539 *Bronzino* is seen at Eaton Wood during June 1959 with an express service. As works no. 2030, the locomotive left Doncaster Works in August 1948 and was fitted at this time with the Kylchap chimney and blastpipe along with multiple valve regulator, being the first of the class to be so fitted as the decision was taken to fit the apparatus before the construction process had advanced too far. Picture courtesy Colour Rail.

*Opposite above*
Blaydon depot was established to the east of Blaydon station, on the north side of the line, at the start of the 20th century to supply locomotives for transporting goods and minerals to and from the extensive Blaydon Sidings and Blaydon Colliery, which was a short distance away. Heaton's no. 60539 *Bronzino* is seen at the shed on 24th May 1961, perhaps after working a goods train in the area. The locomotive was based at the aforementioned from new until October 1961 when relocating to Tweedmouth. Photograph by D.J. Dippie.

*Opposite below*
Gresley A3 Pacific no. 60084 *Trigo* stands under the mechanical coaler at Leeds Neville Hill shed on 27th November 1951, whilst no. 60539 *Bronzino* is on the north eastern side, appearing to have already been under the monolith judging from the large blocks of coal in the tender. There is no indication of what type of train had brought the locomotive from the north east, but this was likely a passenger service at this time, with a smaller chance of a freight; the large Neville Hill goods yard was adjacent to the shed. Both have subsequently survived the many closures inflicted by BR and are used for DMU maintenance and repair, along with storing various types of stock. Picture courtesy *Yorkshire Post Newspapers.*

BRONZINO
60539
60539

60539

# *Tornado* out and about

*Above*
*Tornado* on the A1 near Boroughbridge on 19th August 2008. The locomotive is heading south to the Great Central Railway for test-running to commence. Picture by David Tillotson courtesy The A1 Steam Locomotive Trust.

*Below*
No. 60163 back on the rails at Loughborough and ready to begin testing, September 2008. Photograph by Andy Pratt courtesy The A1 Steam Locomotive Trust.

*Above*
A4 Pacific no. 60019 *Bittern* was to work the King's Cross to York section of 'The Coronation' railtour in mid-May 2009 but was unavailable, allowing *Tornado* to substitute. The engine is seen heading the Up train on 18th May 2009 at Arksey, north of Doncaster. Picture by Hugh Parkin.

*Below*
*Tornado* with Royal Train at Preston on 4th October 2010. Picture by Geoff Griffiths courtesy The A1 Steam Locomotive Trust.

In early 2011 *Tornado*'s boiler was removed from the chassis and returned to DB Meiningen for repairs to be carried out on the firebox. The boiler is seen departing for there from York on 14th January. Picture by David Elliott courtesy The A1 Steam Locomotive Trust.

The boiler in the workshop at Meiningen on 25th January 2011. All the firebox stays were replaced during the visit and new firebars were also installed to increase air flow. Picture by David Elliott courtesy The A1 Steam Locomotive Trust.

Arriving back in York on 8th April, the boiler has since been refitted to the chassis and is having the clothing plates put back into position on 26th April. The decision was taken during this maintenance to repaint the locomotive in BR green livery with early emblem. Photograph by David Elliott courtesy The A1 Steam Locomotive Trust.

*Left*
On 4th April 2012 *Tornado* took 'The Cathedrals Express' from Peterborough via London to Salisbury. Pictured at Huntingdon on the return leg around 22.30, the locomotive also worked several other routes with the service throughout the course of the year. Photograph by Adam Cundick courtesy The A1 Steam Locomotive Trust.

*Below*
No. 60163 arrives at Wansford station on the Nene Valley Railway on 5th April 2012 when the engine spent a weekend working trains on the line. *Tornado* would return in August 2016 to celebrate Wansford's centenary and at this time *Tornado* was rededicated to RAF Marham which is home to several Tornado squadrons. Photograph by Ian McDonald courtesy The A1 Steam Locomotive Trust.

*Above*
*Tornado* was at the head of the Royal Train for a third time on 23rd July 2012. The locomotive was used to convey HRH The Prince of Wales to Alnmouth where he began a visit to the area. No. 60163 is seen at Durham. Picture by Geoff Griffiths courtesy The A1 Steam Locomotive Trust.

*Below*
At Ropley station, Mid-Hants Railway, 26 Feb 2012. Picture by Steve James courtesy The A1 Steam Locomotive Trust.

*Above*
In September 2012 the decision was made for *Tornado* to wear BR blue livery. The first coat is being applied here at Southall on 26th October 2012. Photograph by David Elliot courtesy The A1 Steam Locomotive Trust.

*Below*
Supporters of *Tornado* view the locomotive in BR blue for the first time at Didcot on 25th November 2012. Picture by Ian McDonald courtesy The A1 Steam Locomotive Trust.

*Above*
No. 60163 at Holme on 'The Cathedrals Express', which ran from Peterborough to Winchester on 10th December 2012. *Tornado* finished the year having put an additional 13,500 miles on the clock (taking the total over 60,000) and only 1,590 miles were not completed on the main line. Photograph by Ian McDonald courtesy The A1 Steam Locomotive Trust.

*Opposite above*
On 7th July 2015 *Tornado* and BR Class 55 'Deltic' no. D9009 *Alycidon* were rostered to haul 'The White Rose' between King's Cross and York. The diesel locomotive took the down train, whilst no. 60163 took the up service, which was the first service worked after overhaul, and is seen here halfway to Doncaster at Great Heck. The railtour was run a short time after the death of Sir Nicholas Winton, who helped over 600 children to escape from the Nazis just before the Second World War, and he is recognised through the inclusion of the flags of the Czech Republic and Britain on the bufferbeam. *Tornado* had previously headed the Harwich to Liverpool Street section of the 'Winton Train' which had run in 2009 between Prague and London to celebrate the 70th anniversary of the original trains. Photograph by Andrew Southwell courtesy The A1 Steam Locomotive Trust.

*Opposite below*
In October 2014 *Tornado* returned to Darlington for an intermediate overhaul which saw the locomotive stripped down to the frames and refurbished; in the six years since construction around 80,000 miles had been accumulated all over the country. When reassembled the engine was returned to LNER apple green livery and has run in this condition since; achievements along the way include working the first scheduled steam passenger service on the Settle-Carlisle line in early 2017 and officially reaching 100 mph on test a few months later. No. 60163 is seen here running more sedately at Goodrington with the up 'Torbay Express' on 18th June 2017; Class 66 no. 66012 is unusually positioned behind the locomotive due to the fire risk. Picture by Robert Sherwood courtesy The A1 Steam Locomotive Trust.

THE WHITE ROSE
60163
BRITISH RAILWAYS

60163
BRITISH RAILWAYS
66102
EWS

# Bibliography

Allen, C.J. *Titled Trains of Great Britain.*
Griffiths, Roger and John Hooper. *Great Northern Railway Engine Sheds: Volume One: Southern Area.*
Griffiths, Roger and John Hooper. *Great Northern Railway Engine Sheds: Volume Three - Yorkshire and Lancashire.*
Hawkins, Chris and George Reeve. *LMS Engine Sheds: Volume Five - The Caledonian Railway.*
Hoole, K. *Rail Centres: York.*
Knox, H. *Haymarket Motive Power Depot, Edinburgh 1842 - 2010.*
Mullay, A.J. *Rail Centres: Edinburgh.*
Pike, S.N. *Mile by Mile on the LNER.*
RCTS. *Locomotives of the LNER Part 2A: Tender Engines - Classes A1 to A10.*
Rogers, Col. H.C.B. *Thompson & Peppercorn: Locomotive Engineers.*
Townend, P.N. *Top Shed.*
Yeadon, W. *Yeadon's Register of LNER Locomotives: Volume Three - Raven, Thompson & Peppercorn Pacifics.*

---